DR. DONNA DANNENFELSER

GAME On!

What I Learned During My Time as the Shrink to the *NY Jets* - How to Achieve Anything You Want in Life!

GAME ON!

*What I learned during my time as the shrink to the NY Jets
- How to Achieve Anything You Want In Life!*

By Dr. Donna Dannenfelser

Cover Design by Melodye Hunter
Typesetting: Zonoiko Arafat
Copyright © 2015 by Dr. Donna Dannenfelser.

ISBN: 978-0-9961446-7-4 (p)
ISBN: 978-0-9961446-8-1 (e)

Crescendo Publishing, LLC
300 Carlsbad Village Drive
Ste. 108A, #443
Carlsbad, California 92008-2999

www.CrescendoPublishing.com
GetPublished@CrescendoPublishing.com

To my amazing grandbabies,
Colin, Juliette, Jack, and Christopher

– *"May you always believe in your power
to create."*

A Gift from the Author

The lessons contained in this book are a culmination of my professional experience, real-life transformations I've witnessed, and my own personal journey.

It is my hope that you find your own inspiration, guidance and personal growth within these pages.

To assist you along your journey, I am including a complimentary **keynote audio**, which you can download here:

http://www.drdonnad.com/game-on.html

This is my personal gift – from me to you. *Enjoy!*

Acknowledgements

I acknowledge with much love:

My family, who have been on my team from the beginning, and who will be by my side till the end...you are my life.

My friends, who surround me with their unconditional love, laughter, and unending support.

My wonderful readers, who inspire me to share my life experiences.

And to all those who are struggling, you have the power to rise above any and all obstacles that present themselves to you, if only you *believe.*

Table of Contents

Introduction

Find the Love in

Everyone You Meet

Introduction

Make no mistake: the gladiators that play on the gridiron every Sunday afternoon are extraordinary human beings. They were born into our world just like everybody else, but they grew taller and thicker, ran faster, jumped higher, and focused more intently than the rest of us. They have a special talent, and they use it to entertain millions of people like you and me. I had the pleasure of working with these exceptional men for six years as the Mental Health Clinician for the New York Jets. I learned a great deal in this time, not only during our one-on-one sessions, but also through my experience getting the job in the first place. Over time, I've shaped this knowledge into ten core beliefs—which I'll get to later in this book—as the means by which everyone—and I mean everyone—can build their dream life from the ground up.

Through my time with the Jets, I gained valuable insight into all types of people and discovered the common ground we all share. Every Sunday during football season, I rode on the bus provided for the players' families and looked over at the players' bus, studying their solemn faces. As fans of every nationality, age, and gender laughed and tailgated outside the stadium, the players sat in silence, mentally rehearsing the plays and strategies they had practiced again and again.

Because many of these players came to therapy sessions with me every week, I knew what no one else in this frenzied crowd did: *I knew what they were thinking.* I knew they were mentally turning themselves into our version of the gladiators of yesteryear. Recalling the many films of the opposing team they'd been made to watch, and the hours of coaching that had been burned into their minds.

I knew that, beneath the bravado and bulky muscles, every young man on that bus was worrying—worrying about doing his best, getting the plays right, staying focused on the game, and above all, not getting hurt. Even though they were among the strongest, fastest, and most in-demand athletes in the world, they still faced the same insecurities and self-sabotaging behavior we mortals fall prey to before a job interview or first date, which was a huge part of what I'd been hired to combat.

With my techniques for conquering negative thinking and using positive imagery to create desired results, I helped them to manifest the best possible outcomes. And so what did they do when they started worrying? They flipped their thoughts around and focused on what they wanted to happen on that field instead of their fears. And they did so as a means of accomplishing one of my basic core beliefs regarding success, whether it's a touchdown, corner office, or happy family life: *Dreams do come true if you believe in your ability to achieve them.*

The average NFL career lasts between two and four years, and that's the high estimate. If they last more than eight years, they're considered a superstar. And one thing is for damn sure: no one escapes without permanent injuries. Whether it's to their back, shoulders, knees, nervous system, or state of mind, there is a physical cost for the big money they earn. Even if their body somehow escapes permanent damage, their personal life takes the hit. It's tough out there, and our men on the field know it. And yet, none of them would have given up their spot on that bus for anything in the world. They'd achieved their dream, and they were going to make the most of their shot at NFL glory. Supporting them to do so was a great privilege, and in our weekly sessions I began to synthesize what I'd learned during a lifetime of living on my own terms, and decades of helping clients to be their best selves. I formed the foundation for this book there—in the advice I gave them and in the takeaways from our sessions that I turned into core beliefs I used in my own life and in the sessions I had with other clients.

Now, through this book, you'll gain access to these core beliefs that can lead you to become a successful, fully realized person living your dreams, rather than letting anyone else tell you who you should be. I'll include plenty of examples of how these beliefs worked for the elite athletes I had as clients. And I'll tell you how they fed my own story, which has been far beyond the norm for a woman of my background. Again and again, I'll show you how these anecdotes prove we need people, so if we pick the team that believes in our dream, we'll never go wrong.

My time with the Jets was truly a transformative experience for me. And although you wouldn't know it from looking at me—a Long Island mother of three who'd been called "Barbie" way before I was called "The Doctor Phil of Sports" by the *New York Post*—it was a job I was meant to do. I then expanded my work with the Jets into a highly specialized private practice, providing therapy to some of our country's most elite professional athletes, actors, politicians, and businessmen. In doing so, I honed what I was coming to see as the basis for a dynamic, satisfying life.

From there, practicing what I preached and drawing on all ten core beliefs I'd put together for my clients, I translated my story into *Necessary Roughness*. This hit TV show, based on my life, aired on USA Network for three seasons. It may sound easy, but staying focused while waiting for the universe to line up my eventual success took a lifetime. I had to be patient and believe that everything happened for a reason: the good, the bad, and the ugly. None of this would have been possible without learning how to take a moment, breathe, and understand there are no mistakes, just opportunities that present themselves to us if we keep our eyes open and our minds clear of the negative self-talk with which we all live. More core beliefs right there.

As a housewife turned public school counselor and administrator, international motivational speaker, and adjunct university professor, I'd already pushed the boundaries of what I was expected to be, which formed the foundation for my belief that being ordinary is way too boring. And then, by inventing a position for myself at the Jets and creating a television show based on my experience, I broke through completely, embracing all new possibilities and making up a new life for myself as I went. This last bit I did when I was in my fifties, which is how I came to know another truth firsthand: *we are never too old to accomplish anything.*

I didn't do any of this because I was exceptional, like my high-profile clients. I'm just like you and everyone else, and I always have been—except for one quality, which I cannot emphasize enough: *I've continually been the one who defined myself, rather than letting anyone else do it for me.* I never boxed myself in with anyone else's rules. I've always said: "There are no rules except for the ones you place upon yourself."

And let me be clear, I faced plenty of resistance along the way, which was why it remained crucial for me to find the love in everyone I met. I began to look at the naysayers in my life as my spiritual teachers. The more challenges they brought to my life, the better teachers they became because they ultimately gave me insight into myself. Every *no* I received on my journey only made me see how shortsighted and uncreative these people were. It's amazing how many people in the creative industry don't want to think outside the box and are too afraid to push on a great idea. But when producers told me *no*, I didn't hear them saying I had a bad idea. I heard, "I can't help you. I'm not that powerful." And I felt sorry for them. Meanwhile, other people whispered in my ear, "Keep going. You have a great idea." Those were the people I needed to retain in my life. Either way, I thanked them all for their part on my journey and wished them well on theirs.

Whenever people hear the story of my life, they always want to know one thing: *how'd I do it?* The short answer is the belief I've always had in myself, and what I can accomplish. The long answer is contained in this book: my journey so far, and the ten core beliefs that can help anyone redefine themselves and achieve what they thought was impossible—until now:

1. Find the love in everyone you meet.

2. Never let anyone define you or tell you that you can't do something.

3. Don't be ordinary; it's way too boring.

4. Focus on what you want, not what you don't want.

5. Don't forget to breathe.

6. You are never too old to accomplish anything.

7. Be grateful for where you are in life; you're exactly where you need to be.

8. Be patient, knowing that everything happens for a reason.

9. You need people, so pick the team that believes in your dream.

10. Dreams do come true if you *believe.*

Whether playing in the NFL, juggling multiple jobs and family responsibilities like I did, or facing life's challenges, our core beliefs are what make us a success, or not. Nothing else really matters. How we do it, who we do it with, or when we do it are all trivial in comparison to the power of our belief system. I believe the core beliefs that helped me to achieve my dreams can work for anyone. But we all have our own belief system, and what really matters is to *believe.* People label things *impossible* because they haven't seen anyone do them before. If we can see it in our mind's eye, we have already begun to make our dream a reality. That's how athletes do it. That's how I did it. And that's how everyone who reads this book is going to do it!

Chapter One

The No-Cleavage

Rule

-1-

I've always had a no-cleavage rule when it came to work. But when I dressed for my meeting to tell the New York Jets' athletic trainer what hypnotherapy could do for his players, you bet I wore stilettos. Not those little ones either, but big, high stiletto heels, and a fitted skirt that fell just above the knee. As I've always said: "If your beauty is the thing that gets you in the room, go with it, but always remember that it's your intellect that will keep you there." See, I wasn't going to let anyone define me. It was the 1990s, and just because I was prepared to succeed in a man's world didn't mean I was going to dress like a man, or do anything to cover up my natural assets.

Giving hypnotherapy to the New York Jets wasn't something I had exactly planned on doing, but when I got the call from the universe to go in that direction, I pursued my new goal as if it were one of my lifelong dreams. Early on in my life, it had become abundantly clear to me that there is a force higher than myself that operates in the shadows and makes itself known if we just pay attention. In the same way that I followed the crumbs sprinkled by the universe to this dream job and this amazing time in my life, what happened to me can happen to anybody—if you believe in your power as a creator, whether we call it divine intervention, the universe, or life's force. Whatever your word for it, I am confident it exists. For all of us. The question is: how do we recognize it? And more importantly, how do we tap into it? I've literally spent a lifetime mastering this skill, and my job with the Jets is the perfect example of how I made it work for me, and how you can do the same.

My path to become the Mental Health Clinician for the Jets actually started with my drug of choice—a double tall, white-chocolate mocha—at the Starbucks near my home on Long Island. I was driving from my job as a high school administrator at a local school to my job as a psychotherapist, which I conducted in my home office. My private practice was in a 5,000-square-foot Long Island McMansion where I lived with my three kids and the husband I'd married at twenty, enabling me to leave my extremely conservative Italian Catholic household. Life is a team sport, and as with any team, you need teammates. My husband, Buzz, was first on my team. My three kids soon followed.

At this time, the fall of 1998, my husband and I needed money because ... well, we always needed money.

Buzz was a successful salesman in the children's clothing industry. But when he had a boat, he wanted a yacht, and when he had a Lincoln, he wanted a Mercedes, and when he had a 2,500-square-foot house, he wanted a 5,000-square-foot house. With his thirst for a rich lifestyle driving his decisions, it seemed like we were always overextended financially. I guess you could say Buzz was a good example of someone who focused on what he wanted, and boy did he get whatever it was he had in his sights—even if I was the one who, many times, had to figure out how to actually make it happen, or squeeze us out of some tricky situations.

While I was at Starbucks fueling up, I happened to glance down at an open newspaper and read an interview with Bill Parcells in which he said he couldn't get his team to focus. I was having great success hypnotizing athletes, smokers, and dieters in my side business using my program of hypnotherapy, combining hypnosis with cognitive behavioral therapy. I believed that the cutting-edge program I had developed could help the Jets and establish an extremely lucrative addition to my private practice. If I was going to do this work, why not do it for the best of the best? Right there, I picked my new team. Now I just had to make sure they believed in me, too.

I called my brother, Joe, who had played professional football in Italy on Armani's team, the Jaguars, and asked him who I should call at the Jets. He told me to try the head athletic trainer. When I put in a call, the man actually picked up the phone, which I wasn't expecting at all. But I kept my cool, pulled it together, and gave my pitch.

"As with any athlete, performance on the field is 90 percent mental and 10 percent physical, wouldn't you agree?" I said.

Who's going to disagree with that? I thought, continuing before he could stop me.

"That being the case, I've developed a hypnotherapy program that focuses on the mental aspect of performance. It can turn your players around so that on the field the distractions of life will disappear," I said. "Is that something you'd be interested in?"

"That sounds really interesting," he replied. "I would love to hear more. Call me back in two weeks."

Well, it wasn't a *yes*, but it wasn't a *no* either, and as long I don't hear a *no*, I'll keep going. In fact, even when I do hear a *no*, I keep going. I don't accept it, which is the first of my core beliefs. Don't get me wrong—of course I get insecure. But there are no mistakes in life, only opportunities to learn and make situations work for you.

I definitely grew nervous when I called the athletic trainer back in two weeks, and he told me to call back in *another* two weeks. This happened again, and again, and again. It became months of, "Call back in two weeks." But I wasn't about to give up.

It's all about not letting your ego get in the way, an idea that Buzz brought to my attention as I sat on my front porch one night wondering how long I should wait for this trainer to call me back. The answer? You wait as long as it takes. Of course, waiting is the hardest thing to do because our ego starts playing the "what if" game with us: *What if it never happens? What if I'm wasting my time? What if I wait and it's a no anyway? What if they don't like me? What if somebody steals my idea? What if somebody better comes along, and they go with that person instead?* My answer to all of that is: "What if it all works out exactly as you have planned or even better?"

So, bottom line: *don't let your ego get in the way.*

I certainly didn't let my ego intrude. Instead, I allowed it to figure out how I could push forward. I believed I needed some sort of reference to help legitimize my program and myself. My brother, Joe, appeared regularly on *NYPD Blue*, so I called him with my pitch.

"Hey, would you be willing to help me out?" I said. "Can you call the Jets' trainer and tell him how I worked with you to mentally prepare you to play football in Italy? And how well it worked for you?"

"When did that happen, Don?"

"C'mon Joe, help a sista out."

Joe made the call. Not only was the trainer impressed that an actor had contacted him in the first place, but he was even more impressed when Joe gave him a reference for me. In fact, Joe built me up bigger than life. When Joe called me back, it was with good news.

"He'll be calling you—don't worry," Joe said.

I wasn't worried. If anybody could convince somebody of something, it was Joe.

Meanwhile, Buzz had told his weekend-warrior friends what I was up to, and they could not have laughed harder. They told me I knew nothing about the game of football, nor did I ever watch it, nor did I even appreciate sports. They were right about that. They told me there was no way an NFL team was going to let a woman near their players. Well, we'd just have to see. Bill Parcells hadn't met me yet.

There were plenty of moments when I could have listened to their condescending remarks and given up. Sometimes I doubted that I was ever going to get the athletic trainer on the phone again. I have negative thoughts, along with the usual self-doubts, but I don't let them stop me. I keep going, no matter what. Here's why: *because it works.* I wasn't going to let anyone define me or tell me no—certainly not those knuckledraggers, who had no idea what my capabilities were. I knew what I could do, and I was going to do it. It was then that I decided, once and for all, that the "what if" game would never get the better of me.

By that point, I'd already shaped my entire life with this approach: *when in doubt, DO.* It's how I'd married at twenty, even though my mother had tried to forbid me to tie the knot so young. I told her if she didn't want me to have sex out of wedlock, she'd better find me that wedding gown, and soon. Of course, Buzz and I had already been intimate—it was the '70s—but I needed to get my mother on board with my plan, and I knew that comment would get her there. Let me tell you, she started planning my wedding. Twelve months later I was married.

Buzz and I began our life together in the basement apartment of his mother's house. I wanted our own place. Having a garage door as your front door can be a little jarring, especially when you want to hang a pumpkin on it for Halloween. My first child, Jason, was born thirteen months after our wedding, and by this point I *really* wanted that front door. So off we went, house hunting. A realtor took one look at Buzz's income and told us all we could afford was a shack in somebody's backyard.

While Buzz reeled under this blow to his ego, I concocted a scheme to sidestep this small-time realtor, who'd tried to define who we were and where we could live. I crunched the numbers and went to a different realtor with a plan: given that my brother would be living with us and paying us rent (not true, but who was going to check?), we'd be able to afford a mortgage on a little more than a shack. And I landed us our first mortgage and home. Truly, we wound up buying a 1,000-square-foot house that was *one* step up from a shack. We were stunned when moving day came, and as we entered our new home, now empty of the previous owner's furniture, I noticed that the flooring in the living room didn't meet the walls, and we could see right down into the basement. Ugh! You know what you do when you buy something like that? You rebuild it. But without money, that's a pretty tough task.

To make it work, Buzz got a second job, and I found ways to earn money in the little free time I had while raising my two sons. Yes, Jonathan was born a year later. I was pregnant for eighteen months out of the first three years of my marriage. Fertile, you say? Yes, I was!

My aunt was an Avon Lady, so I sold Avon. I sold jewelry—my jewelry, my grandmother's hand-me-down jewelry, anything I could get my hands on. My philosophy: *where there's a will, there's a way*. If it stood still, I looked to sell it. And then, a woman approached me about selling erotic lingerie. Something told her I'd be really good at this job—it could have been those stilettos; I think I was born wearing them. As it turned out, she was right. Denise became one of my dearest friends, and she helped me start hosting ladies' lingerie parties—at my house, their house, the park, wherever; it didn't matter. If you were a female, I convinced you that you needed to be erotic. I actually made a lot of money in erotic lingerie. I think it was the chocolate penises that sold out every night. Go figure. Now mind you, at this point I was only twenty-five years old with a bachelor's degree in psychology, but I was driven by my desire to rise above any situation I felt was holding me down. If I was faced with a problem, I went at it head-on, with my thoughts going directly to possible solutions.

That personality trait showed itself in many ways that I marvel at, even today. The shack we bought as our first home was between two houses that sat higher than ours, and every time it rained, our backyard flooded and turned into a pond. The ducks from the nearby park would fly in and swim around until the ground eventually absorbed the water. Sure, it was great for the kids to have ducks swimming in their backyard, but as a young homeowner, not so much.

Behind our house, a new strip mall was being built, and I watched as they dug out the soil to pour the foundation. If only I could convince them to bring this dirt to my house and dump it in my backyard, I could raise the dirt level and put an end to the accumulation of water. It didn't take me long to figure out that my stilettos could do the trick in this case as well. Yes, I put them on, with a pair of short-shorts, and I bounced my way over to the construction manager.

"Hey, sir, maybe you can help me?" I said.

Between my smile and my explanation of my situation, we struck a deal. I would let him park his dump truck in my driveway overnight so that it would be safe, and he would dump a load of dirt in my side yard every day. And so he did. The only downside was that Buzz had to wheelbarrow the dirt into the backyard every weekend. After a month of that, he came to me.

"Enough with the dirt drops," he said. "Another load of dirt, and I'm going to bury you in it."

He'd had enough of the manual labor. By that point, our backyard was higher than our neighbors' yards.

They weren't as happy about this as we were, but our problem was solved.

Just do it. That's how I approached everything in life. It's how I became Dr. Donna when I decided to turn the loneliness I'd begun to feel in my marriage into a doctorate degree and a meaningful career, instead of turning it to another man. Over the years, Buzz and I went through the normal heartaches that many marriages experience.

My daughter, Noelle, was born four years after Jonathan. And that year, seven years into our marriage, I found out that Buzz had cheated on me. Of course, he had all the excuses a man who steps out of his marriage can muster. The apologies came. Tears were shed on both sides. I was heartbroken, devastated, and I wanted nothing more than to get away from him. But I was a twenty-seven-year-old mother of three with no career of my own. Where would I go? I stayed because I thought it would be best for our family, and even though I hate to admit it now, I still loved him. We somehow worked through the infidelity and saved our marriage. To be honest, I pushed our relationship to the back burner and forged forward, believing he loved me, staying focused on the good stuff, and hoping things would get better.

A few years later, life actually was better. Buzz had started his own business and was making significantly more money, so we decided to move into a bigger house: a 2,500-square-foot colonial, my dream house since I was a little girl. Could we afford this? According to Buzz we could, but who ever really knew with him? The bigger the better, as far as he was concerned, and I wasn't going to fight it at this point. So we settled into our new home.

One day a tile man came to replace the floor tiles in my bathroom and happened to tell me that I had the cleanest toilet he'd ever seen. I was thirty years old. Now, a clean toilet is important, but I was a college graduate who'd been reduced to a full-time toilet cleaner, and I wasn't even getting paid. It felt like a switch flipped in my head. I saw I needed a career of my own. I had a psychology degree, which I realized was useless without further education. I threw my energies into going back to school and finding a job that was meaningful to me.

Now here is where my story takes an interesting turn and reveals the reality that there is a greater force at work than often meets the eye. We don't learn about it in school. We get a little of it in church. But I'm going to serve it up to you with a twist. It's the same energy force that pushed me to the Jets and that eventually got me to move to California; it's the invisible "something" that finally aligned all the stars and manifested the television show based on my life; it's even the necessary ingredients that made me sit down and write this book.

So there I was, thirty years old; my kids were eight, seven, and three; and I was facing the fact that I needed to go back to school and find myself a career. But what career? There were so many choices. At the same time, I was a mother of three, with a husband who owned his own very demanding business, leaving him little time to be home with his family. First challenge: childcare. Not that big of a problem. I've got a great mom who has always believed in education, and she was thrilled that her daughter wanted to continue hers. Okay, babysitter: check.

I know, I thought, *I'll become an attorney and fight for women's rights. Awesome! LSATs here we come.* I bought the review books and scheduled the tests. All good, right? Wrong. Although I signed up to take the law exam three times, each time, there was a problem.

First time, the test was canceled.

Second time, the place where I thought the test was being given was the wrong location.

Third time, the appointment time on the application was wrong.

I say three strikes, and you're out, and so does the universe.

Okay, so that's not meant to be, I thought. *Simple, just change direction and keep on going. I like to write, so I'll become an English teacher, and during my summer vacations, I will write the next great novel. Hurray! Awesome visual.*

I applied to Hofstra University, and they told me I was in if I took two English classes at a community college, so off I went to SUNY Farmingdale. I was waiting in line to register for the classes—a long line in the parking lot of the campus—and the sun had gone down by this point. When it was finally my turn, I got to the window and learned that both classes were closed for the semester. *Really?!*

As I walked out to my car, I took a deep breath and looked up at the dark sky with all the stars twinkling, as if they are laughing at my plight.

C'mon!! You don't want me to be a lawyer, I thought. *You obviously don't want me to be an English teacher, although that novel I am now* not *going to write would have been awesome. I leave it up to you to show me what you want me to do.*

I got into my car and drove home. Even as I did, I had the strangest feeling that, somehow, my life's mission would be shown to me. I had not a clue as to how, or where, or by whom. But I felt calm, and I believed that the specific details weren't a problem at all.

About a week later, a letter arrived at my home from Hofstra University stating that they were sorry they couldn't enroll me into their English master's program, but I had all the classes I needed to go into their counseling education program. *Ahhhh,* I thought. *You want me to be a school counselor? Hmmmm, I could do that. Yup, that would work out perfectly.*

I loved psychology. I'd be working in the school district, which meant my hours would mirror my kids' school day, with summers and holidays off. This could definitely work—even better than I could have planned. A year and a half later, I received my master's degree. Soon after that, another letter arrived for a substance-abuse program at the local psychiatric hospital. Then another letter came for a clinic given by Albert Ellis, the founder of rational emotive therapy. After that, another letter came from The Harte Center for Clinical Hypnosis.

So, there I was. I had taken out the student loans necessary to earn a master's degree in education with a specialization in school counseling. I had taken additional courses and become a substance-abuse counselor, and then, after even more courses, I earned a certificate as a hypnotherapist, and then, I'd had the privilege of sitting with the renowned Albert Ellis as I took his practicum in order to specialize in rational emotive therapy. Shortly thereafter, I became a nationally certified counselor, which enabled me to receive third-party payment from insurance companies. The girl in stilettos was on a roll—a roll orchestrated by the United States Postal Service, some may say. Only, I knew better.

All good and ready to go, and yet, here again, I hit another wall. I needed a job. So I did all the necessary groundwork. I sent my resume to tons of schools and ... nothing. Schools on Long Island start the day after Labor Day. It was now the Thursday before Labor Day weekend. No job. I got home after a long day at the beach with the kids, who were now ten, nine, and five years old. I walked into the house and grabbed the ringing telephone. It was the secretary from Western Suffolk BOCES, a vocational school, calling me about a school counseling position they were looking to fill *that day*.

"I just got back from the beach," I said. "Can I come in next week?"

"The principal is leaving for the weekend in two hours," she said. "Can you get here now?"

Well, of course I could. I threw the kids to my neighbor, slipped into a suit, pulled my sand-filled hair into a French twist, disguised the salt air on my body with perfume, and raced to the school, which was fifteen minutes from my home, only to realize I'd forgotten to bring along a resume. The only one I had was a crinkled printout in the backseat of my car with a kid's sneaker print on it. *Oh well, this will not stop me,* I thought.

I met with the secretary, told her my sad story, and showed her my crinkled resume. She eyed me up and down. I didn't know if she approved of me or not.

"Love your shoes," she said.

I sighed a breath of relief. Thank God for stilettos. She made a copy of my resume so it looked fresh.

The interview went well, but the principal told me that they'd already put a call in to another candidate, who had not yet called back. If he didn't call before the end of the day, the job was mine. Guess what? He didn't call back. I got the job! Coincidence, you say. I say: not. There's a power greater than ourselves at work in our lives, if we pay attention.

I began to trust that the plan unfolding in my life was even better than any plan I could have put together on my own. The timing was perfect. The situation was perfect. The universe knew everything I needed to land that job. It was later divulged to me that the item on my resume that had clinched the deal during that interview was my substance-abuse certification. It had been no easy task scraping together the funds for that class at the time I took it. There was actually a point when I thought it would be too much of a financial strain on the family to spend the money, but something made me do it. Nobody ever told me that it would eventually make all the difference in securing a job. But, instinctively, when the flyer came in the mail, I absolutely knew I needed to go for it. I had no idea why. I just knew it had to be done. Was it a gut feeling, or a sixth sense, or just a door that opened that I felt the need to walk through? Whatever the case, something greater than myself got me to take that course.

This was the same feeling I had that day, years later, in Starbucks when something made me look at the opened newspaper, and I read the article about Coach Parcells. I was never interested in the sports section of the paper, nor in sports, for that matter. It was the same feeling that made me call the Jets' trainer and believe that I could land a job there. We all have our own name for this feeling. And, actually, it doesn't matter what we call it, as long as we acknowledge its existence and listen to it when it speaks to us.

Fast-forward five years from that fateful post-beach job interview: now thirty-five years old, a school counselor with my own private practice, I was in a much different place than I'd been at twenty-seven. It's difficult to get over an infidelity, and with Buzz staying out late at night entertaining clients, things became strained between us again. Buzz and I separated for several years, yet after I'd tried being a single mom and doing the dating thing, I realized I wasn't ever going to find that *perfect* man; I thought, who better to help me raise my children than their own father? Again, nothing was more important to me than my family, and truth be told … I still loved him. Ugh. That love thing … sometimes I think if it weren't for love, life would be a little more stable—at least for me.

Two years later, and back in the marriage, we were again onto a bigger and better house: this time, one with 5,000 square feet, our third home. As with the previous two, on moving day, I handed Buzz the key to open the door for the first time, thinking the same thing I had the last two times: *it would be so cool if he turned around and carried me over the threshold.* He never did. I contented myself with the consolation that it didn't really matter to me who opened the door. He needed the power; I didn't. I was born an empath, what can I say?

Even with me working full-time and then some, and Buzz working harder than ever, we seemed to always be chasing after money. Buzz wanted a certain lifestyle, but as a commissioned salesman, he never knew what he would be earning from month to month. I was the good wife who used my income to fill in the gaps and decorate our houses to the hilt. It would actually be this 5,000-square-foot house in a gated community that would teach me about being a rock-solid businesswoman. As with all the lessons in my life, I learned it almost by accident and on the fly, when Buzz's income came up short and nearly left us homeless.

We'd been living in this house for four years when one day, Buzz came to me with shocking news.

"In thirty days, I'm not going to be able to pay the mortgage," he said. "I don't know what I'm going to do."

I didn't scream. I didn't cry. I didn't panic. Instead, I immediately went to my computer. I wrote up flyers that said we were selling our house. We lived in a gated community, and I told my kids to stick them in everyone's mailbox. One of our neighbors soon called and said he had a friend who wanted to get into the community. They came to view the house, and as they did, a call came in that I let go to the answering machine. It was another buyer who was interested in the house and asked to see it as soon as possible. The buyers heard every word the person said on that message. What are the chances of that? Was it luck that someone called at that exact time? Or was it that higher power orchestrating things behind the scenes, for both me and that buyer?

All I know is that after that call, the buyers gave me a check and said they wanted to go to contract that week. The negotiation for the house was up and down, but I stayed firm on what we wanted, and we closed shortly thereafter. We worked out a million-dollar deal, and thankfully, financial disaster was averted. Not only that, but in the four years we'd lived in the house, we'd also made a $400,000 profit. And yet, when we closed the sale, Buzz was angry.

"Why are you so angry?" I said.

"Because I feel like I lost."

"You feel like you lost? You could have lost that house. You made four hundred grand in four years of owning this house and you're pissed off?"

There is a silver lining in every disappointment if you look for it. The silver lining for me in all of this was that I gained a great deal of confidence from figuring out how to squeeze us out of circumstances like that. We became good at flipping houses, and I became good at thinking on the fly. The key is to remain calm, no matter the crisis. If you get angry, you make mistakes because you're not thinking clearly. Plus, there's no benefit to being angry. When we almost lost the house, I knew Buzz already felt like a piece of crap. I didn't need to reinforce it for him. I just focused on the good stuff, saving the family and moving forward—always forward.

Every time I fixed something it gave me power. I learned how to solve problems, make deals, and never let on how nervous I'd been during the negotiations. After we'd gotten out of yet another scrape, I'd look back and think: *How'd I sit at that table and pick up my water without shaking? Where did that strength come from?*

I knew that if Buzz had been a different kind of husband, I might not have had the experiences that turned me into a fearless warrior. I know for sure I wouldn't have been as driven in my career as I was. This drive, when paired with my confidence, made me unstoppable. Which was how, all those years later, and now four months in, I still hadn't given up on working with the New York Jets. But I was getting frustrated, and so I called the athletic trainer's bluff.

"I get the feeling you're not really serious about this because I've been calling you every two weeks for four months," I said.

"Oh, I've been busy," he said. "And we've been away, and we're right in the middle of the season."

"I get it," I said.

And then I had a brainstorm.

"Do you drink coffee?"

"Of course I drink coffee."

"What time do you have coffee?"

"Eleven o'clock."

"What kind of coffee do you drink?"

After he told me, I finally let him in on my plan.

"Okay, I'm going to bring you your coffee on Tuesday at eleven o'clock."

"Okay."

"Okay?"

"Yeah, okay."

That's when I put on my stilettos and my above-the-knee skirt and went to my first meeting at the Jets' home office. As I drove onto the lot surrounded by high hedges and pulled up to the main entrance gate, I had to stop for the guard and give him my I.D. He lifted the gate and told me to have a good day. I giggled. I was going to my first meeting with the New York Jets. *Game on!*

It felt completely surreal as I sat in the waiting room looking at all the football memorabilia, including pictures of famous players from the past, most of whom I didn't know. I only knew they were from the past because the pictures had yellowed over time. The trophies were there, too. Articles about players and coaches filled my senses as I read as much as I could as quickly as I could before I was called into our meeting. *This is really happening,* I thought. *This job is already mine. I just have to figure out how to keep it.*

Finally, with two coffees in hand, I entered the trainer's office. I told him everything I'd been doing in my private practice and the success I'd been having with my groundbreaking hypnotherapy program and athletes. He told me he'd have to think about it, but I could tell he was genuinely intrigued. We exchanged business cards, and it was all very professional. And then, as I was walking away, something made me turn around. He was looking at my ass. *Whateva works.*

Now, I could have become insulted because he was looking at my butt. I could have thought to myself that he wasn't taking me seriously. I could have felt "lesser than" for being a woman. Sure, lots of women would have felt demeaned and frustrated, but that would have been because they were interpreting his actions as a reflection of who they were. My perspective on other people's behavior is that what they say and do doesn't say anything about me. It only tells me about them. My reaction to his behavior was: "Got him," and so I had.

The athletic trainer called me the next day and asked me to prove my skills. My first task was to use my hypnotherapy program to address some issues he was facing. *Okay, let's do it.* I was successful, he was convinced I could help his players, and my time with the NFL began.

It was one thing to land the job, but did I have what it took to do the job? I believed so. There was just one problem. It was okay that I didn't like football, but it was going to be an issue that I didn't know *anything* about football when a player mentioned his responsibilities on the field, and I had no idea what he was talking about. My brother, Joe, the former football player, was now living in California, so I had him teach me about the game—by fax (it was the 90s). One day, well into our lesson, we were talking on the phone.

"I really dig the way they have the American flag on the back of their hats," I said.

"What hats?" Joe asked.

"You know ... the guys ... what they wear on their heads."

"Helmets, Donna, helmets," he said.

I knew nothing about football. I mean I really knew *nothing*.

"If there's a defensive line, why aren't they holding the ball?" I asked. "Aren't they defending it?"

"Okay, let's start at the beginning," my brother said.

"Who designed their uniforms, and how unattractive—the tights I mean?" I said. "Although, they sure do outline their butts nicely."

"Donna, FOCUS!"

I had two weeks to learn the game of football and sound like I knew what I was talking about. I wasn't worried. I've always been a quick study, and I'd already gotten in. Most importantly, I knew I could really help these players. I believed I was born to do this. And it was at this juncture of my life that I decided that no one would ever again tell me that I couldn't do something. It was clear: all I had to do after I set my mind to a task was to take one small step every day that would move the energy closer to my goal, and eventually, it would happen. I was now ready to be put to the test. *Universe, bring me my first gladiator.*

Core Belief: Never Let Anyone Define You or Tell You That You Can't Do Something

From the moment my mother tried to tell me I was too young to get married at twenty, through the moment the athletic trainer for the New York Jets nearly gave me a tacit *no*, I never let anyone decide who I was supposed to be or how I should get where I was supposed to be going. Not only that, but I went to the very people who'd first been prepared to foil me and my dreams, and I turned them into the allies who ended up helping me do what I'd intended to do all along. And if those people hadn't been convinced, I would have found other people who were. Why? Because I truly did not let their less-than-enthusiastic reaction to my plan in any way impact my opinion of that plan or my own worth.

You can apply this core belief in your own life by getting real with yourself: Why are these people saying *no*? Does their response diminish the quality of your dream or goal? If your plan does need to be adjusted, in what way should you do so? Or is there another way to convince these people to help you with your original plan? If not, whom can you go to next?

Bottom line: *never take* no *for an answer.*

Chapter Two

Don't Let the Blond Hair Fool You

-2-

Okay, I still had a few more hurdles. Unlike my regular clients who sought me out because they wanted therapy, many of these players had been mandated— sometimes by the court, sometimes by their coaches, sometimes by the head athletic trainer—to come see me. Again, it was the late '90s and therapy was still on the down low. So when a player called before his first appointment, my biggest challenge was convincing him to see me because he didn't want to be in therapy at all. Whatever was going on with him, I had to be able to explain how coming to me would benefit him. I had to very quickly make him believe that I had tools to help him be a better player, a better husband, a better father. I knew that changing his thoughts would change his life, and I had to get him to believe it, too. As long as he made ı appointment, once he came through the door, I knew I could deliver therapy that would be helpful to him.

My usual pitch was that they were "extra ordinary" people, and that even though their issues were the same as the average bear, they were facing them under the spotlight. And when you're an extraordinary person under the spotlight, you need extraordinary treatment, which was what they were going to get during therapy with me. When they heard that they were "extra ordinary" people, it got them every time. Doesn't everybody want to hear that? The ego is amazing.

Then, the next challenge was to keep them coming, and in order to do that, I had to get them to trust me. I had to let them know I wasn't going to tell their coach what they said, or tell the next player who came in for a session, or even let anyone know they were seeing me at all. I was very aware that trust has to be earned, and I was proud when they did eventually trust me.

Now the *real* challenge actually came from within the team itself. I found out that the athletic trainer was encouraging players to come meet with me in the following way: "Just go talk to her. She's easy on the eyes."

I hated when he spoke like that because these were kids in their twenties, and now they came to me thinking they were going on a date, or expecting a free-for-all with a happy ending or something. Even though I was never opposed to using ones looks to open the door to opportunities, in this case I felt it could hurt the counseling process. I needed to play that part down, I couldn't let any of them define me as the sexy therapist who could be laughed off as a lark. I knew I'd earned my spot working with the team, and I was going to prove it. So I had to very quickly cut through that nonsense. To begin with, I often dressed differently with these players, opting for more conservative clothes, less makeup, and a simple ponytail that showed flirtation was the last thing on my mind. Even still, I remember one player coming in wearing black leather pants, a black leather vest (no shirt), and cowboy boots.

"Hey, pretty lady, what ya got for me?" he said.

I had to think quickly about that one. I showed him his police report for beating up a guy in a bar and said, "Just trying to keep you out of jail, dude."

Another player had his own kind of swagger.

"I get every woman to sleep with me," he said.

"Well, this is going to be the first woman you've come across who won't sleep with you," I said.

Even when the come-ons weren't so overt, the players were often out of bounds.

One guy gave me a knowing look. "Whatever you say, hon," he said.

"We're not here for that," I said. "You can't call me 'hon.' I'm not 'hon.'"

Now I was the one to give him the knowing look.

"What we're here for is you've got to stop getting into fights off the field," I said. "Because they're going to suspend your ass. So let's start talking."

Within the first fifteen minutes of their arrival, I had to change the tone of the session by getting them to stop fooling around and respect me. After I was able to accomplish that, the therapy itself had to be quick, too. They had to be ready to play—and win—the following Sunday. A lot of expectations—and money—were riding on their ability to pull it together in time to be gladiators on the field. Working with athletes didn't allow me weeks of sessions to talk about what happened in their childhood. Of course, we might touch on that, but really I was focused on turning them quickly by addressing their immediate problems.

It wasn't just my players who had a change of attitude when we began working together either. From the moment my first football player entered my office, I knew this job was no longer about the money for me. It was about the human condition and the fact that we all want to be loved and respected for who we are, not what we do. It immediately became clear that these men were in emotional pain. And from there I realized that, surprisingly, we were much more similar than I would have ever thought. The conversion of our two worlds happened when I realized they were as soft and vulnerable on the inside as I was. At the same time, my work with them helped me to realize that I was as strong and determined on the outside as they were, even with my hair and nails and stilettoes.

This led to a real ah-ha moment for me: We are all athletes, players on the field, only the game we play is called life. It's here that the stakes are the highest. The practices are short, or nonexistent, and the quarters could last for decades. In this game, the opponent is not necessarily another team, but rather the conditions in which we place ourselves. You see, life is all about choices and the consequences of those choices, much like how a football play can lead to either the scoring touchdown or not. And just as with any athlete, our success is 90 percent mental and 10 percent physical. The coaching we find for ourselves is as important as in any sport because, just like on the field, our internal vision of the end game is what will make all the difference for us.

As you can see, what began to happen was a self-perpetuating loop: as the life lessons we discussed in my office were distilled into my players' strategic football maneuvers on the field, they were also translated back into life lessons for me, which I then brought to bear on the conversations I had with my players and other clients.

Even though I was treating the players so that they could perform better on the field, most of our sessions really had to do with the game of life, too. The issues they brought to my office often had very little to do with football and more to do with everything else. What makes a player lose his focus is as common as what makes you and I lose ours: family issues, marital issues, financial issues, work issues, relationship issues, parenting issues, the catastrophication of the future, or ghosts from the past.

When it became difficult to keep these larger-than-life warriors in therapy, I always used the same line: "Life shouldn't hurt, and if it does, we can do something about it." In order to help them, I knew I needed to convince them that they were warriors in life, as well as on the playing field. To do so, I asked them a simple question.

"So what do you do when you're getting your ass kicked on the field?"

"I dig in, become more focused, and fight harder," they all said.

They visualized themselves overcoming the opponent and winning. Well, of course that worked for them because changing our expectation of how events will turn out gives us the power to keep going and, yes, change the outcome. There it was right in front of me: *life is 90 percent mental and 10 percent physical.*

I started experimenting with this concept. We all have that fateful phone call we don't want to make because we catastrophize the outcome. Well, what happens if we turn it around and visualize a successful phone conversation? If we close our eyes before making that call, take a couple of deep breaths, visualize that the outcome will be exactly what we want it to be, and even feel ecstatic because the call went so well, and we got what we wanted? That's what athletes do. They visualize the plays as successful, and then they go and do it. I tried this approach over and over again, and guess what—it worked! I extended my experiments to other patients, and they found success, too.

A new question arose for me: why don't we do this naturally?

Because we are afraid.

Yes, fear is immobilizing and can keep us stuck in a place of non-activity.

Athletes aren't afraid of the game, and even if that fear should sneak up on them before or during a play, they push it to the back of their minds, focus on the job they need to perform, and then go and do it. And if they didn't succeed, there was only one reason for that: they let their ego get in the way. That's when they were sent to see ... *me*.

So the next stage of the process for me was to learn about the nature of fear for the athlete and how they can master this emotion. My discussion with the players went like this:

"Fear is nothing more than 'false evidence appearing real'," I said. "So what story are you telling yourself?"

"What are you talking about, Doc?"

"You're afraid of something, so what are you afraid of?"

"I'm afraid of failing," they said. "What will the press say? What will my teammates think? Will I be put in second position, or worse, get cut from the team?"

Let's translate that to you and me. If I fail, how will my family feel? What will my friends think? Will I lose everybody's respect? Will they leave me? We are afraid that failing at something will be more painful than not trying it at all. So we stay stuck where we don't want to be just because it feels safe, it's familiar, and we were often told early on to stay with what we know. Many people are not doing what they want to do in life because they are afraid of failure. It is a well-known fact that the person who believes they can succeed, and the person who believes they cannot, are both right.

The person that believes they cannot succeed is powered by fear, and it gets in the way of everything. So they stay stuck, they are unhappy, they become disappointed with themselves and their lives, and they bring their frustration and unhappiness to bear with everyone they meet. It seeps into all they do and all they talk about. Then, their belief system takes a hit, and they become negative-vibration sources in all their encounters. Before long, people leave them and move on to more positive entities. I can't open my dream business because I may fail. I shouldn't get married because it may end in divorce. I shouldn't buy that house because I may not be able to pay the mortgage. I shouldn't write the book because it may not sell. The *should not*'s go on and on.

But there's an antidote. The question to ask yourself when fear consumes your thoughts is: *what would I do if I weren't afraid?* Then hold on to your answer, visualize what you would do and how it would feel. Believe you have the ability, the universal support, and the innate wisdom as a creator to achieve your goals. All people who are successful in life take gambles. They never doubt, and if they do, they push through anyway. They never quit. They never let anyone get in their way, and ultimately, they never lose. That's how athletes do it. That's how I did it. And that's how you can do it, too.

There it is. The purpose of the sessions with my athletes was to realign their belief systems to match their desires for the future, to inspire each and every one who entered my office to realize their potential and have the strength to go out and score that touchdown.

You never know what words will turn a person around. For me, it was the tile man who inspired me to go back to school, and now, I'd become everybody's metaphorical tile man, pushing them to realize their potential. So began my role as the nontraditional therapist, turning my clients around in a New York minute.

Many players also struggled with aggression issues, which were even more difficult to navigate while living under the constant scrutiny of the media. Football is a very testosterone-driven sport. Most of their hours were spent hitting each other very hard in exchange for a great deal of money, and in order to do that, they needed to go to a place of intense anger. After they'd successfully connected with their rage on the field, some players had trouble controlling that emotion in their private lives. And there's the rub. They needed the power of what we call controlled anger or aggression, but once they'd gone deep inside to find it, some had a hard time using the switch that's supposed to control it. Much of our work together focused on this process and learning the tools required for mastering their emotions, on the field and off.

Of course, this isn't just an issue for NFL players and other professional athletes. How many of us have anger that sometimes gets the best of us? When things come flying out of our mouths at the most inappropriate times, the damage is done, scars are made, and pulling it all back together becomes very difficult. The first step to controlling these emotions is to understand them.

Anger is a response to being hurt. First we get hurt, and then we get angry. On the field, this process works just fine, and the game of football could not be played if these players couldn't make this emotional jump. Anger on the field is used to drive the player forward, no matter how much pain needs to be endured. But how well does anger work in the game of life? Not well at all, unless it's an emotion that causes us to move forward in a positive direction. Anger in life is good if it gives us enough energy to change circumstances we find intolerable, no matter how painful the process of change may be. Anger does have a purpose off the field, but only if it is directed to improve situations. For example, it's positive when we get so angry at our circumstances, knowing we are totally responsible for them, that it causes us to do something that brings us closer to our goals.

Sometimes, I had to get original with my therapeutic interventions. I had one player who'd had difficulty in school and found it hard to remember all the plays outlined in the team's extraordinarily thick playbook. I knew that one of the tips for improving memory was to use memory hooks to organize and retain information. He was a womanizer, so I knew what his memory hook would be.

"Okay, this is what we're going to do," I said. "We're going to go through the playbook, and you're going to visualize every play with the players being different ethnicities of females. So for this play you're going to visualize all the players being Asian women in their little thongs, lined up the way they have to line up for this particular play. And that's the way you're going to remember every play."

We did it that way, and yes, he remembered every single play. As I sat in the stadium watching him play, I recognized the lineups and yelled out in my mind—*It's the French girls! Run the French girls—no not the Swedish girls, the French!*—as if telepathically he would hear me. And as he finally ran the plays correctly, I took my seat and breathed a sigh of relief thinking: *It's working. It's really working.*

Sometimes the intersection between the NFL and therapy took as much getting used to for me as it did for the players. I was at practice, and one of the coaches was preparing to speak. Suddenly, there was a loud CRACK. I jumped and then looked around me, trying to figure out what had happened. The players barely seemed to notice. Well, the coach had broken his clipboard over his leg, just to get their attention. I was like, *Really? Was that necessary? Can't you just say, "Hey, all eyes up here?" You had to break the clipboard on your leg?*

Getting me to go to the games was yet another negotiation. My therapy was working well with the players, so well in fact that the athletic trainer thought it would be invaluable for me to be at the games. Now remember, I was in this for the mental health of the players. I wasn't an avid football fan, and to sit and watch a game for four hours was not my thing, so when the trainer told me I had to be at the game, I balked.

"I don't think that's necessary," I said.

"Yeah, it is," he replied. "Fifty-yard-line tickets ... how can you turn that down?"

"It's winter, and freezing, and I'd be more comfortable at home watching it in the warmth of my living room."

Yeah, I thought, *in my house where I can go in and out of the room at will.*

We all know that football minutes and real time are two different things. Did you ever wait for four minutes of a football game to pass? It could take an hour! Just like life, when you're in a waiting period for anything. Waiting for that job offer to come through, or that promotion; waiting those long nine months for the baby to be born or those long months leading up to your wedding; waiting for that perfect house to present itself as you're out house hunting; waiting to recuperate from surgery or a severe illness, and the list goes on and on.

So what do you do when you're waiting? Well, athletes practice their plays, they strengthen their bodies at the gym, and they watch hours of postgame screwups and successes, studying their opponents. And that's what we should do during those excruciating waiting periods in our lives, too. We should prepare for the future game, or in our real-life equivalent, our next big event. Prepare for what is ahead, and then allow the universe to do its job as it aligns all that is necessary for you to move forward.

There's definitely a mental component to this process, too. During times of preparation, most athletes act "as if": as if they are the star of the team, as if they have already won the playoffs and are getting ready to win the Super Bowl. They act as if it has all worked out exactly as they wished it would. Being an athlete gives them the knowledge that they have the ability to make that touchdown; they've done it a thousand times before, and they can easily do it again when, of course, they are in the zone.

The zone is a special place for an athlete. It's where all is perfect, and they hear nothing other than the sound of the stadium full of fans cheering for them. Their focus is on nothing other than scoring that play, and they believe with every cell of their being that they can and will achieve their goal. They become one with the field, one with the football. Everything is in perfect sync, perfect harmony. Nothing can go wrong, and it doesn't. It's that belief and confidence that can make us a winner, too. It's the difference between successful people and those who are not. I know you're thinking, *Well, sure, but how do you do that?*

Answer: Act "as if." We need to get into the zone, people! Act as if your dreams have already manifested. At first, it may feel like you are lying to yourself, but try looking at it as preparing for your future. In other words, don't dress for the job you have today; dress for the job you want tomorrow. Those in authority will notice you, and your life will change. You are intentionally moving the energy toward your goal because you have all the physical power you need to get what you want. You just need to use it.

Do you want love in your life? Start by loving yourself. People are attracted by those who are lovable. Act as if you are in love. Be in love with life, the future that's on its way, the people you will be meeting who will introduce you to your perfect mate. Be the person you want to love, and love will find you.

You want to be happy? Do just that: be happy. What do athletes do to act "as if"? They relax, breathe, visualize, and believe they've already achieved.

The trainer for the Jets definitely acted "as if." One day, I came home and found a big box on my doorstep. The return label read: New York Jets. *What could it be?* It was clothing to keep me warm at the game: a Jets jacket, gloves, scarf, and two tickets. How could I not go? The trainer acted as if I had accepted his invitation even though I had not. And guess what? He got what he wanted. I attended the game, and I was warm, thanks to his clothing gift, sitting in the family section under the warmers on the fifty-yard line.

This brought up a bit of a quandary for me. Now that I was going to the games, there was the issue of acknowledging that many of the players knew me. They didn't want anybody to know that they knew me because that would tell everyone they were seeing a shrink. It wasn't information they wanted out there; again, it was the '90s. But I knew acknowledging them was important, so I left it up to them. What began to happen was that each player had his own hand signal to show his acknowledgement of me. One hit his chest with his fist. Another gave me the two-finger salute off the top of his forehead. Another rubbed his chin. It was adorable and so respectful. I realized then that I had become a significant part of these players' lives, and I loved it. They became my boys. From that point on, that's how I referred to them. Yes, nontraditional therapy for sure.

My new job was an adjustment for my family, too. Since I worked with the players at my home office, I sat my kids down before my first client ever came over.

"There's going to be some professional athletes coming in and out of the house," I said. "And you're going to see them, but you can't go and tell anybody who you've seen, or what you've seen because it would really blow their confidentiality. It would get out that they're seeing a therapist, and it could become very uncomfortable for them. So we're not going to tell anybody that I'm doing this. But I wanted you to know because you're going to see it."

So, of course, all three of them ran up to their rooms, got on the phone, and excitedly told their friends the news. They were so bad at keeping secrets. I tried my best to keep the identities of the players secret, but with each passing day it became increasingly difficult. I made sure I hid my datebook and gave no indication as to who was seeing me for therapy. But even still, teenagers are very resourceful.

One day, I was working with one of my clients. Behind him was a window that looked out onto my backyard. As we were talking, I watched over his shoulder as my son, Jason, jumped up in the air and came back down, again and again. I realized he was jumping on the trampoline, trying to look in the window. As I attempted to keep my face totally neutral, I next saw his brother, Jonathan, jumping up and down. *I'm going to kill them*, I thought.

And then my daughter, Noelle, jumped up. I watched as her face registered shock, and then fear, as she fell backwards off the trampoline. I couldn't help myself. I gasped.

"No really, it wasn't that bad," the player said. "I didn't feel like that at all."

I tried to act natural while worrying that Noelle had broken her arm. Or worse. As soon as he left, I went into our family room, and she was sitting there with an ice pack on her ankle.

"I'm going to kill all three of you," I said. "Take down the trampoline!"

There was so much to get used to with these players. First of all, their size: these guys were huge. They stood between six feet and six feet eight, weighing in between 200 and 360 pounds. Once, while sitting in my office, I noticed that a player's thigh was the width of my hips. When I shook their hands, my hand seemed to disappear in theirs.

Of course, that could mean only one thing: they ate a lot. Since I saw the players in my home, Noelle was assigned to answer the door and let the players sit in the family room till I got to them. And so she did. One night I was running behind, and a player came in to wait for me. Noelle welcomed him, and he took a seat in the recliner in front of the TV. Buzz came home moments later with a pizza for dinner and walked in to find the player jumping up from the recliner while handing Buzz the remote. I guess there *is* honor between men when it comes to the remote. Why am I surprised?

Anyway, Buzz, being cordial, told him not to worry about it and offered him some pizza. Then he realized there was only one pie for three kids and a monster of a man. From then on, Buzz always bought two pizzas, just in case.

When my kids grew a little older, we got into some even stickier situations. I had one client who wasn't supposed to set foot in a bar. The league called and told me he'd been seen at a bar, and I had to bring it up during our next session. When I confronted the player, I couldn't believe his response.

"It's come to my attention that you violated one of the agreements you made by being in this bar," I said.

"Your son told you I was there," he said, obviously angry.

"My son?"

"Yeah, the tall, skinny one. That little weasel ratted me out?"

Jonathan wasn't supposed to be in a bar either. He wasn't old enough.

"What are you talking about?" I asked.

"We made an agreement we wouldn't tell on each other."

"My son, Jonathan, was at the bar?"

"Wait, how'd you find out then?"

"From the league."

"Oh, oh."

When I confronted my son, he was just as mad.

"I can't believe he told you that," Jonathan said. "I lived up to my end of the bargain."

Nobody had gotten hurt that night, and I was eventually able to laugh at the coincidence that had brought the two of them together at the same bar after they'd already crossed paths at my house. But some of the situations the players got themselves into were much more serious. And while I'd first thought of the gig as a lucrative moneymaker, I soon saw these extraordinary young men like my own children. They were young and vulnerable, and I became very protective of them. While they are our modern-day gladiators, they're also human beings, but they often get treated like million-dollar stallions. So they became very important to me. I knew I was doing my job well when a player's mom came over to me at one Sunday game and whispered in my ear, "Thank you for saving my son's life."

I never looked at my work as saving a young man's life, but I guess I had. My approach became more personal that day, and any therapist will tell you that's not a good thing. Professionally speaking, a therapist is not supposed to become emotionally involved with her clients. It can cause psychological transference of emotions if one's not careful. I became very careful and very aware. It was tricky because most of these players were from out of town, and if they were single, they were living here without their families. If they were married with children, their families were usually with them, soothing the situation, and sometimes making it worse. Many times, my home was the only safe haven where they felt comfortable. Boundaries were blurred. Yet how can you work with a team and not have it affect you personally? Who are we kidding when we say we won't let feelings get involved? I felt, they felt, and the conversion grew deeper.

My nontraditional therapy approach became more nontraditional over time. When I had a player who'd just kicked drugs and was going to be alone on Christmas, I made sure he knew there was a present under my tree for him. As far as I was concerned, it was better for him to come to my house than let the emotional stress of the season trigger him to use drugs again.

I also got so much from my players. I could see myself, and my circumstances, in some of their stories, and I learned a great deal from their reactions to what was happening in their lives. These guys were often on the road for games, requiring them to be away from home a lot, and they all had the same complaint:

"I have to go out of town for a game, and my wife gets mad because I never call. I don't call a lot when I'm on the road because when I do, she's always complaining about my mother, or she's complaining about the kids, or she's complaining about whatever broke at the house that week, and the conversation sucks and leads to only one thing … a big-ass fight."

As a salesman, Buzz was often out of town for work, and he wouldn't call me either. Suddenly, I knew why. *I do that. And my husband neglects to call me when he's on the road as well.*

And then it dawned on me. We needed a women's workshop. If I didn't know why my husband didn't call me, then the players' wives and significant others didn't know either, and they should. Shortly thereafter, women's workshops were the talk of the team. Interestingly enough, some players didn't want their wives to go.

"What?!" I asked.

"Yeah, some of the guys are a little concerned that the wives will get together and tell some stories that shouldn't be told," the trainer explained.

"I can make sure that doesn't happen. Is Parcels in support of the workshops?"

"It wouldn't be happening if he wasn't."

"I promise you it will help. You guys need to trust me."

And so they did. Soon, four weeks of two-hour workshops were on the books. And so, my time with the women of the NFL had begun.

At least twenty-five women attended, all lovely young women, some wives, some significant others. And that's where I saw that there was a pecking order: there were the seasoned wives of the NFL and the newbies. Yup, the first-string wives and those who were not. It was interesting to find out that when the team was losing, the wives got along much better, pulling for each other and, in their own way, raising moral. They instinctively knew their role when the team was on a losing streak. But when the team was winning, there was an air of competition among them. They began to notice who was receiving the better gifts from their spouses, and like in all communities, gossip hurt a lot of goodwill. All of this was quite normal for an intimate organization of this type.

I heard a lot of anger from these women. Most of them knew what they had signed up for by getting involved with a professional athlete, yet they were young, most often having left their families and support network behind while they followed their husbands out of state. There was anger, resentment, and loneliness. I ordered a book for them, *The Dance of Anger*, by Harriet Lerner. It helped, and we kept working together.

I learned so much from my players and their significant others. The players' complaints about their wives helped me to see my relationship with Buzz in a whole new way, and much closer to the way he saw it. I could hear my voice in the voices of these young women, and I started trying to see my own experiences in the same way I told the players to approach theirs. By doing so, I changed my thoughts, and yes, I changed my life. I was less concerned with trying to control things. I was happier. I felt more present.

Core Belief: Don't Be Ordinary—It's Way Too Boring

There's an old saying: Take the road less traveled. For some, it seems too difficult. But if you're at a stage in your life where you're bored or feel you can't stand your current life anymore, it's your body telling you that you need more. It's up to you to decide more of what, but you need to understand that you're done with your current life. You need to discover more about yourself, the world, and the others in it. Trust your body and—trust me— you'll become excited about life again. Now, some may say this is being selfish. Well, I challenge that idea: If I'm not happy, I can't do a damn thing for anybody else. I become resentful and filled with a yearning to be anywhere else. That said, should you hurt people in the process of achieving your dreams? Of course not, but many times, it's not about leaving others behind. It's about moving forward, and taking those you love with you.

Where can you find places in your own life to look beyond the ordinary and become extraordinary? Or, start from the other end: what's not thrilling you now—at work, or at home? What could be changed within the existing parameters of your life? Or do you need to transform yourself completely and take on an all-new job or romantic relationship? Why settle for being bored when you can challenge yourself and find all new possibilities, abilities, and joy? No, really, that's not a rhetorical question. Why are you settling?

Chapter Three

Your Life Would Make a Great TV Show

-3-

At this point, I was juggling four demanding jobs. I was a school administrator, university professor, motivational speaker, and I had a private practice, spending most of that time dealing with the Jets. I found myself working eighteen. hour days, and I was exhausted.

Why so many jobs? Because I could. I couldn't turn opportunities down. They were money-generating gifts from the universe, and even more than that, I loved everything about each one of these jobs. They were people oriented. I was a leader, a teacher, an inspiration to those who needed it, and I provided a safe haven for those who needed to be accepted for who they were, not what people wanted them to be. I got a natural high from working with someone and helping them get the strength to rise above their circumstances. It made my life worth living. I was making a difference. My life mattered.

If you are ever depressed and want to get out of it, go help somebody. In order to provide aid to another person, *you* need to rise above what's holding you down. And as you do that and gather the positive energy needed, you strengthen your own inner ability to heal. As a result, you heal yourself as well as the other person.

The interesting twist to all of this was that professional sports is a pretty small niche, and football players know basketball players who know baseball players who know boxers, etc. As a result, I began to get referrals from all arenas of professional sports. That led to CEOs of companies, political personalities, and top-performing actors. The list of people who sat on my coach became very impressive, even to me. People that I'd only read about were contacting me for appointments, and it didn't matter who they were or the power and prestige they held; the moment they sat on my coach, they all turned into the twelve-year-old from yesteryear, talking about their insecurities and the wrong decisions they made, or the heartache that others caused them. All of it reinforced the notion that *people just want to be loved and respected for who they are, not what they do.* The one thing that they had in common was that they all responded to the notion that changing their thoughts would change their lives for the better.

The biggest challenge in changing your thoughts is identifying the damaging ones, refocusing, and producing positive thoughts. Athletic performance is 90 percent mental and 10 percent physical; so is life. The physical attributes you've been born with don't matter as much as the attitude and belief system you live by. Performance anxiety in sports, or life, spawns itself when a negative vision of your future invades your thoughts. For an athlete this can happen anytime they feel that the game is getting away from them. It happens in life when we feel the control we used to have over money, relationships, children, careers, and our bodies slipping away. You say to yourself, "I used to feel so confident. What's changed?" The only thing that's changed is the way you are thinking. Just like a professional punter who, all of a sudden, can't seem to kick the ball between the uprights. He's done it a million times since he's been ten years old, but for the past four games he just can't do it. If he hasn't suffered from a physical injury, the problem is psychological. Getting to what's keeping him out of the zone needs to be explored. Most often getting at the troubling thought and working through the insecurities associated with it usually does the trick, and the athlete is back in the game, successful once again.

But what about when there is a physical injury? When something truly has changed? Athletes go to rehab and come back on the field or the court or into the ring, and yes, at first they are sluggish, but before long they have regained their strength. Many, if not all, athletes play hurt. Not necessarily injured, but they all physically hurt for one reason or another—just like the rest of us. We all have been hurt at one time or another. The pain I refer to in this regard can be psychological, emotional, and/or spiritual in nature and most often stems from childhood. There is truth in the saying that we spend most of our adulthood trying to get over our childhood. They are our "issues" or "takeaways" from the past that form the mental tapes that play over and over again in our subconscious minds and cause us to behave and think in certain ways. These tapes are the building blocks of our belief system; we base all of our decisions on them. But what if we handled our emotional injuries the same way an athlete handles their psychological recovery?

After an athlete physically recovers from an injury, there is a psychological recovery that needs to take place as well before that athlete is truly healed. Most athletes return to the field still feeling some level of physical pain. Athletes are adept at replacing their body's message of pain with a thought of self-healing. That is the athletic brain working at its best. They convince themselves that the pain they feel is their body telling them that they are getting even stronger than they were before. Their minds have to get used to the fact that their bodies can take anything that comes their way. They build their confidence back slowly as each day they believe they are getting stronger. One day it clicks in that they are strong once again. It may take a while for that confidence to come back, but their belief system tells them that it's inevitable. Teammates help by believing in the player and cheering him on. That's why it's so important to have a strong team of your own. Derek Jeter fools himself into thinking that he was never hurt in the first place. Some may say that's lying to yourself, but are you really lying or just getting in the way of the negative thought and empowering your body to use every ounce of energy it has to bring you back to health? Thousands of research studies have been conducted on how the mind heals cancer patients. There is truth in the power of thought healing our physical bodies, and our professional athletes reinforce that fact every day.

Okay, so we know how athletes on the field do it, but how does that translate to you and me? First, we need to identify our negative thoughts before they have the chance to really take hold of our actions. Our bodies actually tell us when we are having negative thoughts by giving us an anxious feeling in the pit of our stomach. Allow yourself to become conscious of your physical feelings the moment you feel anxious, and ask yourself what you're thinking about. At that moment you will realize that you are having negative thoughts. Then take the negative thoughts and change them. Turn them around to positive thoughts. Or, if you're obsessing over a negative experience, ask yourself, "How are these thoughts serving me? Am I looking to feel sorry for myself? Am I looking for others to feel sorry for me? Am I looking for a reason not to move on with my life? Am I making an excuse not to fulfill my dreams?"

You can shift your thoughts by finding the silver lining in everything and expanding on it. For example, losing a job for any reason never feels good, whether you liked the job or not. How are you going to pay your bills? What will others think of you? It's very stressful, but it's been my experience, personally and in dealing with many of my clients, that most people laid off from work really don't like their jobs anyway, or they have been looking for something better for a while. It's just a way for them to pay their bills, which I know is very important—don't get me wrong. The reality is that you do have the power to make this experience culminate into a better scenario.

I was laid off from one of my school administrative jobs, and as I was being told that the school district was eliminating my position, I laughed—a very inappropriate reaction, I know. Even my boss at the time looked at me and asked me if I was okay. I laughed because I was in a doctorate program at the time, and between work and my family and all that goes into completing a dissertation, I didn't know how I was going to accomplish this goal. I laughed because I realized that the universe was providing me an opportunity to devote all my time to finishing the dissertation. I was very aware, at this point of my life, that there is a bigger force working on the sidelines of our lives, and I trusted that it knew better than me. I trusted that this time spent not working wouldn't last long, and I would gain employment again and be fine. Well, as it turned out, I was laid off in June, collected unemployment, put all my time into the dissertation, got it done by September, got another school administrative job in October, and in November I defended my dissertation and got my doctorate degree. As a matter of fact, I was the first one in my class all because of the layoff that June. "Coincidence," you might say. ... I say not.

I never, not once, allowed myself to accept a negative thought. Now mind you, I didn't say I didn't have them. It's just that if they crept in, I changed them. The choice of focusing on how I could make the layoff work for me was enough to move me into positive thinking. Changing our thoughts to positive ones is something that we have to work at every day. We were not brought up to think in this way, so we need to retrain ourselves. Constantly reminding ourselves to focus on what we want is one sure way to accomplish this new state of mind. Changing your thoughts does change your life. Free will, my friends. We have the free will to choose how we interpret and react to all circumstances that present themselves to us. It's about the perspective you choose to buy into that makes all the difference.

Many people assume that changing one's life is easy for rich people, but the average person, not so much. Is it really? Think about it. Who are "rich people"? The criteria for being rich differs among all of us. If you have a large savings account, are you rich? If you have no debt, are you rich? Is it all about how many toys you own? Rich or not, changing your life is scary in whatever financial situation you find yourself. And to be frank, saying that you are afraid to leave your current circumstances because of money is just an excuse not to do it. If you have money, most often you have more responsibilities and more debt. Most people live above their means. If they earn a million dollars, most often they're spending three million. There are just as many options for lower income people as there are for the wealthy.

Thinking that changing your circumstances is dependent upon how financially secure you are is a limiting thought. People who think with this limitation are looking for a guarantee of success. There are none. That's not how life was set up. The rule of life rests on the following notion and can be proven by all the successful people who started out with nothing and made millions: *belief in a successful life will always lead to experiencing a successful life as you've imagined.* If you believe that only the rich have the opportunity to have happy and successful lives, that will be your experience. Change is disconcerting no matter who you are. You can even look at it this way: the poor have less to lose than the wealthy, so change should be easier for them because they have less to leave behind. The truth is this*: the brave make changes; the fearful do not.* It has nothing to do with income or savings.

With a layoff, you have the free choice to either stress out about not having money, or you can use the time to find something more desirable. And yes, I do hear you screaming from your home, "But will my bills get paid?" My answer is simply, "They will." Somehow, somewhere, you will find the money. Actually, our society is set up for us to have a safety net. There is unemployment and a whole system of social services that could be tapped into if need be. You may not want to go there, but my point is that you will not die. And where there is life, there is hope. There are a million scenarios for making your bad situation better if you allow yourself to focus on that.

Changing your thoughts requires you to focus on a new life by imagining the infinite possibilities that lie before you. I know, you've read all the self-help books, and that's what they all say. And besides, you know you don't want to be doing what you're doing today, but you don't know what you would rather be doing. Well, I'm pretty sure that all of us want to be happy. So if you are at a point in your life where you don't know what to focus on, focus on being happy. Visualize yourself twelve months in the future standing tall, feeling proud, and being in an even better place in your life than you could have ever imagined. Don't just visualize it, but feel what that would feel like and stay with that visual and feeling for a few minutes. You have just changed your thoughts. This is what athletes do before going into that big game. They dig in and focus on the win. If they didn't, they would never be able to complete a play successfully.

The bigger picture here is that it's not about the play; it's about the player. And the same goes for you. If you want to be successful, you need to think success, dress for success, and act as if it has happened. If you don't, it will never happen because you're not focusing on what you want. You're focusing on what you don't want, and because of that, what you don't want to happen is the exact scenario that will manifest. Why? Because that invisible force I've been talking about wants to make your dreams come true, and the only way it knows what you are dreaming about is by locking into what you're thinking about. So focus on what you want to happen, not what you don't want to happen. That's what athletes do, and that's what I did.

I've been asked how a mother of three from Long Island got a TV show based on her life without an agent or a manager. Here's the true answer: I left a secure job (making a lot of money with great retirement benefits), my home, family, and friends, and I said to everybody, "I'm moving to California to make a TV show based on my life." I can still hear my mother screaming from Commack, "Are you out of your mind, child!" I convinced myself, just like athletes do, that I could do it, and I would do it. I had no idea how. I just felt it with every cell of my body that it would happen. It did, but it didn't happen overnight. Nothing like that does. There was a long way to go before the stars lined up for that to take place. I kept my eye on the ball and stayed focused. But first, I needed to attend to those eighteen-hour workdays.

At this juncture my kids were eighteen, sixteen, and twelve years old. When I got into bed at the end of my eighteen-hour day, my legs were often throbbing. Sometimes, when Noelle tried to talk to me after I worked with my clients, I could see her mouth moving, but I couldn't really hear what she was saying because I was still thinking about the issues my clients had spoken about in our sessions. It was a constant balancing act, and I often found myself turning to McDonald's or other fast-food spots to keep everyone fed. One night, after I'd picked up another drive-through dinner with Noelle in the car, she began to protest. "I want a home-cooked meal," she demanded.

"So do I," I replied. "Whose house do you think we could go to?"

"Mom, you're not funny," she said.

I've always felt, you're either part of the problem or part of the solution, so on my way home the next night, I went to the local pizzeria and convinced the owner to put together a program where they made full meals for my family four nights a week. The leftovers made up a meal on the fifth night. I was home on the weekends, so again, all good in the hood. It was easy to convince her to work with me as I spoke about the working mom and how many of us were out there and how this could be a gold mine for her if she presented the program to the community. I could be her test run, at a cut rate, and if it worked, just think of all the side business she could collect from this. Win-win for all.

I did that a lot with people that came in and out of my life. It's about creating a reality that works for you. It's about negotiating a deal: how can the fulfillment of my needs work for you? When you negotiate with that premise in mind, both parties benefit. You become a team. Coaches do it all the time. How can we make this a cohesive team? Something's got to be in it for everyone. How do we make the payoff from the big win work for each and every player?

In between my daytime school administrative job and my evening private practice, I picked up the prepared food, brought it home, and put it on the stove. Soon, I was tucked away in my office with my clients, and my family could come in and eat whenever they were hungry. Voilà, home-cooked meals. I just wasn't the one cooking them. There's no rule a mom has to be a certain way, and even if there were, I wouldn't follow it. Again, don't be ordinary; it's way too boring. By thinking up a new approach that worked for my family, we were all happy, and we all got fed—all because I added another player, a player that would feed us.

This lifestyle had been going on for several years when I went out to Los Angeles to visit my brother, Joe. By this point he was a working actor and had landed a part on *ER*. I was visiting him and decided to do a day in the life of an "actor." That required a visit to the set while he was shooting. When it was time for the crew to move from one lot to another, the director, who had a golf cart, asked me if I wanted to ride with him to the next lot.

"What do you do for a living?" he asked as we drove together.

"I'm a mental health clinician to the NFL," I said.

"Really? Now there's a TV show."

I later told Joe what the director had said. He smirked, "Oh yeah, everybody in California thinks their life would make a great TV show. What makes you think you're so special?"

I shrugged. A few days later, I flew home. I was soon busy with my life again and didn't give our conversation much more thought. Joe, however, started getting phone calls from people who were interested in my story. When he called me with the news, I laughed.

"Oh really?" I said. "I thought everybody thinks their life would make a great TV show. Why don't they call up other people, Joe?"

"You know, maybe we *could* start pitching this," he said.

That's how we got started with the whole idea for a show based on my time with the Jets. Joe was very involved from the beginning. Because he already had connections in Hollywood, he was able to get us meetings and hook me up with potential writers. I began flying out to Los Angeles every few months in order to try to keep things moving along with the show. Of course, there were many people who said they could do stuff that they couldn't actually do, and there were many *no's* for every *yes* we received. But we did receive enough encouragement to let me know our idea had potential. And as I've said, I've never been one to take a *no* seriously. If someone said no to me, it didn't mean I wasn't going to do whatever it was I wanted to do. It just meant I wasn't going to do it with them. And, well, that was their loss. Little did I know at the time, though, this was the beginning of a *seven-year* odyssey to sell the show.

During that time, people had a lot of suggestions for how I should be pitching the material. And they had a lot of negative comments about how there was no way a Long Island mother of three with no agent, no talent manager, and no writing credits was actually going to sell a TV show to Hollywood. But I didn't let them define me or what I could do, and I just kept my eye on the goal, which I knew I *could* meet eventually. Everything else was just information, some of it useful, some of it not so much.

So in addition to my four jobs, I was now pitching a TV show based on my life with the Jets. Pitching a show is no easy task. Okay, so it's based on my life dealing with high-profile athletes, but is it a comedy or drama? A half-hour show or an hour-long show? Well, the answers to those questions depended on the writer involved at the time. Joe and I became a new team, and we needed to gather other teammates for this adventure—writers for sure, but who? It was like betting on a team. All the teams are good, but who's going to the Super Bowl this year? And you need to pick the winner before they even go to training camp. This is when we get into the concept of "allowing." There is a belief in quantum physics that we are all connected, that there is a collective unconscious from which we draw what we need. In this case, it was more about the idea that, "when the student is ready, the teacher will appear." I saw it with my clients, especially one in particular.

Of course, it was the one with the most to lose and the most difficult issues to work through. He was struggling with every disappointment that life could deliver. But when I looked at him, I could always see the good. I connected with his pain as he connected with my hope. His struggle was one that you've heard before, when every three steps forward resulted in two steps back. His progress was slow, but as football is a game of inches, so was his therapy. We focused on the good. If it was one inch forward that we could count on, we focused on that one inch. Little by little, we worked together to battle his demons.

One Sunday, after a long week of difficult therapy, I boarded the family bus to Giants Stadium, and as we were driving along, the players' bus rolled up next to ours. I spotted this player on that bus, and he seemed to be in deep concentration. I worried for him, not just for his success in today's game but for the parts of his past that seemed to be surfacing and distracting him. I had watched throughout the season as his beautiful smile seemed to fade with each day of failure, failure in his personal life and on the field. I wondered if he would ever smile again.

As our buses seemed to line up next to each other, he picked up his head and our eyes met. For a quick moment I wanted to turn away so that he wouldn't see I was looking at him, but I didn't. I could feel his pain, his self-doubt, his fear. Not knowing what to do to get him out of his own head, I held the palm of my hand against the window to show him I was with him. And in that instance, I watched as he slowly, carefully, placed his monster of a hand against his window, mirroring mine. We had connected for that moment. We seemed to exhale at the same time, and then ... he smiled. He played an awesome game that day. It was the day he turned that proverbial corner. And each game thereafter he improved. He got stronger and stronger. He had finally changed his thoughts, and now he was changing his life.

We are all connected—more than you know. You are never alone. *Life shouldn't hurt, and if it does, there will always be someone there to help you.* You just need to get out of your own way, and you do that by changing your thoughts to positive ones.

Core Belief: Focus on What You Want, Not What You Don't Want

Once I had my television goal in mind, I knew it was what I wanted—I mean, *really* wanted—more than anything else in my life, and I stuck to this, even when my conviction was tested again and again as you'll see in the next chapters. The moment you take your eye off the ball, you lose the game. Many of us get distracted by the competition, by the failures, or by the doubtful energy of others. But, really, it's all about focus. That's how athletes succeed, and it works.

Getting into the zone is about feeling—*really* feeling—the success of your dream. Train yourself to focus all your inner energy on what you want, and then, experience the feeling of having achieved it. This is the most important part: You must visualize what you want in as much detail as possible, and every day you must do one small task to move toward your goal. If you want financial freedom, you must visualize that abundance in all its glory. Don't say, "If I could just have enough money to pay my bills, it would be great." No! If you do that, that's all you'll get: just enough. You want it all, right? So think big. Go for it. Why not? It takes exactly the same thought process to manifest one million dollars as it does one dollar. It might take a little longer, but in the end, you will win.

Now it's your turn. What do you want? I mean what do you *really* want? What do you want so much that even if it takes seven—or ten—years to get there, you'll still consider that time well spent? Put your focus on the positive, and you will achieve it.

Chapter Four

My Body Is Crying

-4-

A few years into pitching the show with Joe, I flew out to California to take some more meetings. While I was there, my brother sent me for a massage. I thought this was very nice of him, and I looked forward to doing something for myself. Although I was always reminding my patients of the importance of self-care, I had absolutely no time for such things in my own life. While it's common for therapists to have their own therapist, while balancing four jobs and taking care of three kids and a husband, I didn't have enough hours in the day, and I hadn't been in therapy for nearly a decade. As a therapist, you see people who are in a bad place. No one has ever walked through my therapy door to tell me that their life was great. By the time they got to me, they were in severe psychological and emotional pain. And, as a therapist, I absorbed this pain metaphysically. Without a way to release it, you wind up holding it. Yet even though I was well aware of this fact, I kept telling myself I would take care of it when I got the chance, that I was fine for now.

When I worked as a supervisor in the schools, I always made sure my counselors went out to lunch, but I ate lunch at my desk. I even held workshops entitled, "Who's Taking Care of the Caretaker?" But I was very bad at taking my own advice. On the other hand, everything in my life was running smoothly, so I didn't think much about it.

It was similar to football players who, no matter how hurt they got on the field, they still continued to play. They dared not complain, and that had nothing to do with the inner workings of the NFL; they were just self-driven. I witnessed athletes who played with the flu and would remove their helmets, throw up on the field, and then put their helmets back on to continue playing. I marveled at that. We all know what it's like to have the flu and how you wince at the slightest touch, yet these gladiators would run around a field, getting tackled by opponents at high speed, while suffering from an illness that required them to be in bed. Who would do that? Well, if you're an athlete in life, you do that. Many people will push themselves to the end of the road and wind up getting very sick because they won't take that moment to breathe or attend to their own well-being, whether it be physical or, in my case, psychological. Athletes on the field don't pull themselves out of games. Most often they are forced off the field, and their helmets are taken away to make sure they don't go back on. So would be the case with me, as I was soon to find out.

When I walked into the masseuse's room, she was burning incense, and I could tell she was interested in her patients' spiritual health as well as their physical health. As she was giving me a massage, she began to tell me what she felt.

"Your body's telling me that you don't feed it enough water," she said.

"Oh, okay," I replied.

That seemed like an easy fix. As my massage ended, I realized she'd been able to feel what was going on with me, and I was curious about this.

"So what else did my body tell you?" I asked lightly.

"Actually, your body is very sad because it's telling me if you treated yourself as well as you treat others, you'd be in a better place."

Her words brought me to tears, and once they started rolling down my cheek, I just couldn't stop crying. I called Joe to tell him I was ready for him to pick me up.

"I'm done," I said through my tears.

"What's the matter?" he asked. "I sent you for a massage. Why are you crying?"

"I don't know," I said.

When I got into the car, I told him what had happened.

"She told me that my body is sad because I don't take care of it," I cried. "I take care of everybody else and not myself."

"Well, then, start doing that," he said.

If only it were that easy, right? Over the next year, I was busier than ever, and things got worse. I couldn't watch the news or intensely emotional TV shows or movies because they brought me to tears. If I accidentally caught sight of a sad commercial, I found myself crying. *What the hell is wrong with me?* I thought. *There's no reason for me to be crying right now.*

I could only watch *Star Trek* because it didn't tug at my heart strings. I didn't want to see anything that depicted the worst of humanity. *Star Trek*, for me, was about tolerance and getting along with others, rising above the worst that humanity has to offer. I was yearning for happy endings.

Absolutely anything could set me off. If my mother called me and said, "Did you hear what happened to that little girl?"

"Please don't tell me," I would respond. "Please. I can't take anymore."

One day I was driving home, and I passed a drug rehabilitation center. In the front yard, three men were raising an American flag. As a substance-abuse counselor,

I knew how difficult it was for someone to stay sober, and I respected that journey so much. I started to cry, and not just little tears either, but big wracking sobs as I thought about them raising that flag every day, and how, every day, they had to fight to stay clean when most of us took it for granted that we didn't need a drug to make it through our day.

It was then I realized I had empathy fatigue. I couldn't take any more sadness because I wasn't releasing the emotions I absorbed through my work every day, and it had backed up within me to the point where I was getting sick. The treats I'd once turned to were no longer enough. When I was feeling down, I'd always cheered myself up by dunking Oreo cookies in milk—you know, feeding my inner child. But that didn't work anymore. I had a cyst on my ovary and a twitch in my eye that wouldn't go away. I looked horrible.

I was in Manhasset one day, window-shopping on Miracle Mile, and I walked into a Louis Vuitton store. As I looked around, I knew I could buy any bag I wanted. I could buy five bags, with cash, and it wouldn't even dent what was in my savings account. But I didn't want any of them. I wasn't happy, and I knew a handbag wasn't going to make me happy either. *Wow, what's happening?* I thought. *You've got to get the hell out of here. You've got to get the hell out of here!* I could hear the thought repeating itself in my mind, again and again, but I had no idea what it meant.

Around the same time, my girlfriend, Gerri, had come out to Long Island, and we went to dinner. Gerri and I had been in the same Brownie troop, and we'd been through everything together since then. I knew I could say anything to her. Also, unlike with my family, I didn't have to pretend to be the strong matriarch who had it all together. I felt safe being candid with her about what I was going through without causing any alarm.

"Gerri, you know, I get up for work, I go to work, and then I come home, and then I eat, and I watch TV, and I go to sleep, to get up to go to work, to come home, to eat, to get up to go to work, to come home," I said. "Is this it? Is this what we do until we die? I think I'm disappointed in life."

She gave me just the tough-love talk I needed.

"Okay, what the hell is wrong with you?" she said. "Yes, that's what we do."

"Really?" I said. "And maybe, one or two weeks out of the year we go on vacation, and that's it? That's so messed up."

No matter what she said, I knew there had to be more to life than this. I had accomplished all my goals—and then some—but I wasn't satisfied. This whole time, from 2003 to 2005, I was regularly flying out to California to have meetings about my show. One day, I was driving on the 210 Freeway in California when I suddenly felt like I was driving home. As soon as I had the feeling, it passed. I lived on Long Island, with my husband and family. Not in

California. Where was this feeling coming from? But from that point on, I knew I'd live in California someday. Just because I'd started out as a Long Island girl, didn't mean I had to stay a Long Island girl. The words I used with my clients flew back at me, only they seemed to have more meaning: *"The circumstances that you are born into should never define who you are, what you're capable of doing, or where you will wind up."*

And that's when I realized I was stuck in what I call "Crabs in the Bucket Syndrome." Some call this the rat race, but I saw it as crabs in a bucket. You see, growing up on Long Island allows you to go crabbing. You take a boat out at night, and you shine a flashlight into the water. The crabs see the light and start swimming toward it. As they do, you take a net and scoop them out of the water and put them into a bucket. You never have to put a lid on the bucket because they don't work together to get out. They try to climb on top of each other, pulling the ones before them down, and as a result none of them can escape. They all want to get out, they all try, but they can't. It's kind of what a lot of us do who are unhappy with our situations, whether it's financial, personal, or spiritual. We complain to each other, or what I call have a "bitch fest," and somehow that makes us feel better. You know, misery loves company. We all stay in the bucket, realizing we're not alone. We don't encourage each other to take that risk, to try something never done before, or to just follow our inner navigation system taking us to places we've dreamed of.

People will try to keep you exactly where they are, saying it's safe, making you think you are crazy for even thinking you could do what's never been done before. They will say things to make you feel foolish, selfish, or ungrateful—not because they want to hurt you—but because they just don't know any better.

The problem for me was my life on Long Island was working, at least on the surface. When things aren't working, it's much easier to decide to make a change. But other than the fact that I was feeling unhappy and full of this uncomfortable yearning, my life was exactly as I'd wanted it to be. There was no reason to leave. In fact, even though I was leaning more and more toward California, I didn't see how I could leave New York, and my whole life. All I had to do was keep working another ten years and I could go into retirement without a worry. Yet I didn't feel fulfilled. Something was missing.

In the winter of 2004, Buzz and I went on vacation to Jamaica. I'd brought a book with me to read on the beach, but I couldn't get into it. I was sitting on this gorgeous beach, but I was fidgety, and I couldn't relax. I remembered that the resort where we were staying had this little, old library, so I decided to go find another book. I started looking at the books, and this one book moved. I swear—it moved. So I pulled it out, and it was about successful people that had left their regular lives to go pursue their dreams.

Every chapter was just one success story after another, and there wasn't one person throughout this entire book who'd failed. They might not have done what they'd originally thought they were leaving their former lives to do, but whatever they wound up doing was even better than their original plans had been. By the time I'd finished reading this book and put it down in my lap, I was suddenly very clear.

I'm doing this, I thought. *I'm going to give up everything and go to California to finally sell my show and make it really happen. I would have a major platform on which to spread my belief that, "Life shouldn't hurt and if it does there will always be someone there to help you."* Finally I could see my purpose.

That book had been a major turning point for me, and I desperately wanted to bring it home with me. My first thought was that I'd just take it, but I felt a gnawing sensation that I shouldn't. I decided I'd leave the book I'd brought with me and take the book I'd read, but again, I felt like this wouldn't be right. The book's title was so simple that I didn't even write it down. I knew I'd remember it, and I could buy another copy when I got back to the States. Of course, when I was at home and went to the bookstore, I couldn't remember the name of the damn book. That was okay. It had already done its work, and I knew exactly what I needed to do next. To this day I can't remember the name of that book, a book that made my life's path become so clear, which is so odd, don't you think? But more importantly, once I knew what I wanted, I never lost sight of it again. And that's when I decided to breathe.

Breathing is a two-step process. You breathe in, realizing you have done all you can, and you breathe out, realizing that you need to hand off whatever you're dealing with to that higher power. When you take a moment to breathe, it's your cue that you are giving yourself a moment to relax, and you can take that moment to reward yourself by knowing that you are awesome. And you know that you are awesome because God doesn't make junk. It is in this moment of letting go that you hand it all over to a higher force—you surrender. It's in the surrendering that everything will turn around for you. It's what athletes do. When they're in the toughest spots on the field, they breathe and relax. They let it happen. It's when everything turned around for me. And there are countless stories of others who have had their whole lives change for the better the moment they stopped trying so hard.

I must have heard myself say a thousand times, "We spend most of our adulthood trying to get over our childhood." And whether it's wrong messages told to us in our youth or suffering abuses that were wrongfully inflicted upon us, we have subconscious tapes that play over and over in our minds convincing us of our self-worth and our power—or lack thereof—and the biggest untruth of all: we need to go outside ourselves to find happiness. We need to have that expensive car, or that McMansion, or those designer purses or jeans. Most often, it's only after everything is taken away from us and we are forced to turn inward that we begin to discover the power of our being. It's that "come to Jesus" moment when you have nothing else to give and don't know how to go on. You feel so tired that you just have to give up. We're like hamsters on that wheel of life: we just keep going round and round, never getting anywhere.

What we really want is never "out there." It is always inside our hearts. Athletes go inside to their core to gather the strength, the knowing, and the confidence to complete the play. They never look at their teammates, coaches, or fans to do it for them, nor do they blame them or their circumstances for the situation they find themselves in. You never hear a football player say, "Well, if it had been a sunny day, I would have made that play." Or, "If it weren't for the coach's bad attitude, I would have made that touchdown." When things get rough, they dig in and go to their core, tapping into the strength and wisdom of their higher selves. And most often this happens in the eleventh hour, when most of the game is over, the clock is ticking, and the screaming on and off the field is at its loudest. Winning comes down to seconds on the field and their state of mind.

Just imagine if you could achieve your heart's desire. Do most of us even know what that means? Is your heart's desire that amazing job? That mansion on the water or on a mountainside? Is that what would make you calm and relaxed? Would you trade a million dollars for happiness? Would you trade happiness for a million dollars? Is happiness worth more than money, or is money worth more than happiness? I can't answer for you, but if you're looking for happiness, finding out what athletes do after a victory may help you.

As you're watching a football game, a basketball game, a soccer game or the like, what do you see athletes do after their triumph? They jump up and down and then fall to their knees, they bow their heads, and they look up to the sky. What are they doing? They are giving praise. They become grateful to that higher power that dwells in all of us, that invisible force that organizes those serendipitous happenings.

Momentary happiness is simply the result of achieving a desired goal. Long-term happiness is the result of being grateful. There is a direct correlation between exhaling and gratefulness. You can exhale the moment you begin to look at your life and acknowledge what you're thankful for. Even for the little things, like hot water. Do you realize how many millions of people in the world do not have hot water? Some don't even have clean water, forget the temperature. Start there and you will be overwhelmed by how much you have to be grateful for. That's where it begins, but don't get me wrong—that's not where it ends. This exercise is just to help you get out of your own way. And believe me, I'm no better than you. I use this exercise when I need to get grounded. I even use this sometimes today when I get lost. Yes, I still get lost. And so do our million-dollar athletes. It's part of the human experience. So cut yourself a break because the truth of the matter is that if you don't, nobody else will.

We're looking at the wrong thing when we obsess about money, or the lack of it, and people with money know it. Like I said before, the people that walk through my door are all in pain. I have a high-profiled clientele. If having a lot of money was the common denominator to happiness, I should be out of business and I'm not! So the question is ... can you have a lot of money and be happy too? Well, that's up to you.

If you're at a point in your life where all the things you thought were important don't seem to satisfy you anymore, you need to take a moment. If you don't feel fulfilled as I did, you need to ask yourself if you have a higher purpose. Is there a calling that you have been ignoring your whole life? Something that you've always wanted to do but were told it was silly? And even if you don't know what you should be doing, but know that you don't want to do what you're doing now, that's all you need to change course and go in the direction that best suits you.

First, you need to trust in something higher than yourself, whether that be God, the force, the universe, whatever you talk to when you're all alone. There's an old cliché, "Go where the love is." That's easier said than done. Many people look at that and say, "Well, my family loves me. My partner loves me. I should go to them for my answer?" No, that's not the love it's referring to. The love that's meant in this case is where you vibrate at your highest level. And you know your vibrating at your highest level because you feel hopeful, powerful, happy, and confident that your dreams can come true. You feel at peace. All of those feelings happen after you breathe, relax, and take notice of how far you have come on your journey. Like the athlete who has ten seconds left in the game, he takes that breath, focuses, relaxes his body, and allows himself to go with the flow.

Core Belief: Remember to Breathe

Did you ever put a little kid in time-out? If you have, or if you've seen a kid in time-out, you understand that we put them there so that they can reflect on what they've done wrong, and we hope they will realize there is a better way to handle whatever got them there in the first place. As adults, we should put ourselves in time-out when our lives aren't working for us because this is the place where we can take a deep breath, relax for a moment, and gather our thoughts. We need to reflect. In doing so, we often realize what we are doing wrong, how to make our lives work better for us, and consider revising the past actions that caused us the pain we are now experiencing. It is also at this time that we might consider handing our concerns over to the universe, or that higher power in our life. And in doing so, we can finally exhale. You should try it. You will be amazed at how letting go of your worries often causes solutions to present themselves to you. Let life show you the way, and in doing so, trust your inner voice. You will never go wrong.

How good are you at remembering to breathe? When do you stop and breathe? When might you benefit from breathing more? Are there moments in your regular day when you can steal time to breathe? If not, where and how can you create them? Are there areas where you're stuck, and how can you address them by breathing more? Do you know the benefits of meditating? Is it time for you to learn how to meditate and visualize?

Game On!

Chapter Five

I Love You, but Right Now I Love Myself More

Game On!

-5-

I knew what I had to do, and not just for my show, but also for myself—for my health, my happiness, my overall well-being. If I stayed in New York, I was too successful to slow down. I wasn't going to stop doing any of my jobs. Moving to California meant leaving *several* great careers, all of which I loved—a mental health clinician for the New York Jets; an administrator for a Long Island public school district, with its excellent benefits and eventual pension; and an adjunct university professor, motivational speaker, and psychotherapist with a successful private practice—for a *possible* great career as a creator of a television show. Two years into the pitch process, I knew it wasn't going to happen overnight. I was nearly fifty years old, retirement was within view, and the golden handcuffs felt safe, but I knew

I had to be brave. And I knew I had the power to create what happened next with the way I thought about it.

Even when you know what you need to do, doing it can become complicated. Change is scary when there are no guarantees. And that's why many of us stay way too long in situations that we know have served their purpose or are causing us pain. Sometimes the universe sets up events that take decisions out of our hands and force us to move forward. So it was for me in the months ahead.

That football season, someone within the Jet's franchise realized I had never signed a nondisclosure agreement and asked me to do so. I took a deep breath.

"I can't sign a nondisclosure agreement because I'm going to make a TV show about my life," I said, knowing full well what the consequences would be.

They did not invite me back to work with the team that season, and I suddenly had one less career to wind down. Although the New York Jets had not renewed my contract, many of the players decided to continue seeing me on their own. They'd also begun referring their friends to me; this was when my practice branched out to include many highly successful athletes from other sports, politicians, and CEOs. As with my football players, they were often extraordinary people who lived far beyond most people's everyday existence. I found great satisfaction in helping them to function at an even higher level and discover that their happiness was within their reach. And the more people I helped in this way, the more

I began to see that I needed to do the same for myself. I was redefining myself, and it was working.

But I still had a husband, to whom I'd now been married for almost thirty years, and three children (twenty-eight, twenty-six, and twenty-two years old), all single but still living close to me. I knew what I needed to do, but still, I hesitated. And then, one day, I went straight from my school administrative job to other work obligations that evening. I didn't call Buzz to let him know I'd be late. And then, even though I knew he was already home from work and it was long after I normally got home every night, I still didn't call him. I guess I wanted to see if he'd notice I wasn't home and become concerned. He didn't call me to make sure I was okay, even though it was eleven thirty at night before I finally pulled into the driveway.

No one's looking for me, I realized as I sat in my car.

This realization made me sad, but it also meant I was free. For an athlete, becoming a free agent has psychological advantages as well as disadvantages. You can choose a team of your liking as opposed to having to accept whoever drafts you. You can entertain offers from other teams and decide with whom to sign a contract. You don't have to take what you are given, you don't have to stay where you don't want to, and you have the freedom to choose where you will be going next.

The disadvantage is the fear that comes along with being free. There's always the fear that what you thought would be better for you may not turn out as you thought.

You also have that feeling of being out there on your own. Waiting. And worse than that, what if it doesn't work out?

We all want to be free agents at one point or another in our lives, especially when the pressure of being responsible for others becomes overwhelming and you just want a break. What you do with that freedom after you get it can make all the difference in the world. Well, I had the freedom. I had the excuse. What did I want to do?

Shortly thereafter, I made up my mind. I waited for Buzz to come home from work. While he was going through the mail in the kitchen, I thought, "This is as good a time as any."

"I have something to tell you," I said.

"What?" he said, barely looking up at me.

"I'm going to leave my job, and everything, and I'm going to move to California because I can make this show happen," I said. "I'm not telling you that you have to go with me because you have your business here, and I understand that you have to do what you need to do. But I am willing to walk away if you decide that you don't want to go with me. We can sell the house, and we can split everything, but it's something that I just have to do."

Obviously, he had some questions, and we got into it. We'd had a long marriage, and we'd been good business partners for many of those years. When we'd had a common goal, we'd worked well together and made it happen. But there was one truth that meant even more to me that day.

"I love you," I said. "But right now I love myself more."

It was the first time in nearly three decades of life that I had put myself first. And once I had my new priority in sight, I never, ever let it go, or let anyone sway my focus. Self-love was a new thought for me. A new experience. In the strict, Italian-Catholic household I was brought up in, self-love was the equivalent to being selfish. I don't blame my parents for that; it was a concept that wasn't recognized back then. It wasn't recognized until 1956 when psychologist and social philosopher Erich Fromm proposed that loving oneself was different from being arrogant, conceited, or egocentric. His theory culminated into the philosophy that in order to be able to truly love another person, you needed to be able to love yourself.

Self-love means caring about oneself, taking responsibility for oneself, respecting oneself, knowing oneself, being realistic and honest about one's strengths and weaknesses. In other words, self-love is about connecting with yourself. It's about ignoring the *shoulds* you've been taught and focusing on your needs as well as everyone else's, not focusing on what makes others happy at the expense of your happiness.

As a wife and mother, I willingly took on the job of caretaker, lover, housekeeper, cook, nurturer, social planner, holiday expert, nurse, negotiator, and candlestick maker. But like the old saying goes, if Momma's not happy, nobody else will be happy. You can't take care of anyone else if you aren't healthy and happy. That's why it's true that when one person is sick, two people need help. The caretaker often times needs more support than the person they're taking care of. If the caretaker is not taking care of themselves they will be of no use to anyone else.

Yet still, many of us struggle with this concept. I'm no different, and that's why it took me three decades to take my turn. Many of us stay in situations that are not good for us way longer than we should, whether it be work related, relationships, or environmental situations. And then we look back and are angry at ourselves for doing so. What are we waiting for? It's actually very simple: we're waiting for someone to give us permission to change things up. We tend to look outside ourselves for the answers, for guarantees that we are making the right decision. The answers aren't out there. The answers are within. This means that somehow you need to figure out how to sit quietly and embrace the here and now. As in my case, I had connected with my inner self and figured out what I needed to do, and I was ready to take the next step.

Although Buzz didn't decide to move his life to California, he was willing to accept me moving mine. He had decided that he would commute back and forth, keeping his business in New York while I pitched the show in California. Real estate was booming in southern California at that time, and he saw an investment. We sold our home, made a significant amount of money, and moved all our belongings to a 5,500-square-foot house on the side of the San Bernardino Mountains. My plan was to buy a house with the cash from the proceeds of selling our home as I would no longer be bringing in the money I used to, but Buzz thought differently and persuaded me that we could do this.

"We'll build this house, hold it for a few years, and flip it, just like the others," he said.

It meant that he would need a place in New York as he intended to fly back and forth every weekend. I couldn't see how we would be able to afford two homes. I had no idea how he planned to do it, but he was confident it would work. I stood doubtful, but it was forward motion and that's all that mattered to me at the time.

Now mind you, I didn't make up my mind and move the next day. I had to make a plan, and it took a year to do so. It didn't take long to sell the house on Long Island as we were living on a golf course at this point. We priced it just right and it sold pretty quickly. Buzz and I moved into an apartment in Port Washington for the next year. During that time I saved as much money as I could and readied myself to shut down my private practice and exit from the administrator job. I also gave notice to the university I was working at that this would be my last semester teaching, and I slowly cut back my motivational workshops. All the while, I spent my vacation time that year traveling back and forth to California building my new home, putting every penny we had into it, and trying to wrap my arms around the fact that I was doing the right thing. Scary? Yes!

And then the doubt settled in. Leaving the administrative school job was a big decision. I had been in education for sixteen years by then, and it's where I picked up a significant check at the end of every week, not to mention I had one of the best health-care packages out there with the best security. It was coming close to the end of the school year, and I knew I needed to hand in my resignation. I hesitated and thought, *"Well, what if I kept my job here on Long Island and just spent a lot of vacation time in California. I could have both worlds and stay secure."* I held my resignation letter. And then the universe stepped in. My supervisor came to me that very week and announced that due to unforeseen circumstances they would not be renewing my contract. Oh my God, the decision was taken out of my hands. But even better, I could leave and get unemployment. How awesome! Had I resigned a few days earlier, I wouldn't have gotten unemployment. The universe did me a solid that day and I stood grateful. It also meant I had no choice. I had to go.

Many people have said to me, "But Dr. D., you had money. What about the people who don't have any money to save? We just can't pick up and leave."

My response has always been, "You're not paying attention. I didn't just pick up and go. I made a plan. I found a way. If you don't have the resources, you actually have less to lose and more to gain. You're making excuses!"

There are no guarantees with these decisions. In the game of life, there are those who are players and those who wish they were. There are spectators and fans who stand by the sidelines and watch the players in awe at what they can achieve and are willing to sacrifice for that big win. And then there are those who just don't get it.

I had a cleaning lady named Claudia, and she was from Argentina. Her husband was a factory worker, and both her husband and she worked many hours during the week just to make ends meet. She came to me one day wanting my opinion. She had an opportunity to move to New Jersey and open a water ski and fishing equipment business by the Jersey shore. They would sell their house and put the money they made down on the business. They would be taking out almost a million-dollar loan from the current owner of the business and would have to make a certain amount of money for the next five years in order to pay back the loan. They would be struggling for the next five years and could lose everything anyway, but it was a way for them to get ahead if it worked. They wanted my opinion.

My question was, "If you don't do it, will you regret not trying?" She said yes. I posed a follow-up question. "If you do it and you fail, have you really lost anything but time?"

She answered, "Well, we would lose the down payment on the house, but it's not that much anyway. We wouldn't have any place to live, but I guess we could move in with my parents."

"Then what are you waiting for?" I replied. The first year, it rained every weekend in Jersey. Keep in mind, the business was based on tourism. But low and behold, they made that year's payment by the skin of their teeth. Five years later, they had paid back the loan. I went to see them the year after that. They had just moved into a million-dollar house of their own, and she introduced me to *her* cleaning lady. She had become a millionaire!

Claudia knew I was definitely a player in this game of life, and she wanted permission to take a shot at it. I knew she was a worker, and I knew there was no way she would allow herself to fail. It's up to you to decide if you are brave enough, talented enough, and trust yourself enough not to quit when the going gets rough. But I will tell you this: You have the skills. All you need is to understand the game, to know what it takes to win. The common denominator in success is dedication and a commitment to make it happen. Lack of money is no excuse. It's an element that raises the stakes and keeps you in the bucket with the rest of the crabs. It's at this point that players dig in, focus on where they want to go, and say, "Game on, mother f—"

We moved into our house in California in July 2006. I turned fifty years old. I was close to retirement, and I was starting my life over. This just goes to show you that life doesn't end with your AARP membership. And mind you, I walked away from an awesome retirement, health care, and ten future years of major earnings for something that others told me was impossible to achieve.

I often wonder if I was running away from a life I could no longer tolerate or running toward a dream I believed I could make happen. All I know is that I was running. I was determined, I was excited, and I was fearless. Failing at this was not an option.

I was fifty years old, and the thought of pitching a show without a manager or an agent didn't seem to faze me. I believed I just had to hit the right combination of teammates and I could make this a win. How hard could it be to make a TV show? It would happen. I just wondered how old I would be when it actually came to fruition.

People are always hung up on age. My hairdresser in New York, Kathleen, and I had met when I was twenty-seven years old. We were both pregnant with our daughters when she started doing my hair. She wanted to become a cosmetology instructor and had to go back to school to get a degree. She balked about doing it.

"It's going to take me four years to do that. I'll be old by then," she whined.

"Well, in four years you'll be that age anyway, and you'll either be a teacher or not. How would you like to bring in that birthday? As a cosmetology instructor, or as someone regretting that they didn't follow their heart's desire?"

That fall she enrolled in school, four years later she got her degree, and she can now say, "I am a teacher. I'm doing what I've always wanted to do."

Kathleen had doubted herself, but in my case it was always others who doubted me, just like when I was working as an administrator and decided I wanted my doctorate. I was in my forties, and when I approached my supervisors to sign off on some paperwork I needed, they responded with less than enthusiasm. I heard things like:

"Why would you spend all that money at this point of your life?"

"How old will you be by the time you get this degree? You don't need it."

"It's a lot of work, Donna. Do you really want to put all your time into this right now?"

Keep in mind, none of these people had their doctorate. Was it jealousy? Was it "Crabs in the Bucket Syndrome"? Whatever it was, it didn't stop me. I forged ahead. Why? 'Cause I could.

You're never too old to do anything. Unless, of course, you're posing for *Playboy*, but then again there are some women who have ass-kickin' bodies well into their fifties and *should* pose for *Playboy* and put *that* in the AARP magazine.

There have been a number of players who have played in the NFL at or above the age of forty and have performed like they were still young, energetic players in their twenties. Their passion for the game did not die with time, and their bodies somehow managed to withstand the rigors of the NFL year after year.

George Blanda was the oldest player in the history of the NFL. He retired at the age of forty-eight, just short of his forty-ninth birthday. He played for three teams in his career: the Chicago Bears, Baltimore Colts, and Oakland Raiders. He holds the record for the most seasons played in the NFL at twenty-six. He was a quarterback and played for four decades. He was also a great kicker and continued to kick exceptionally well until he retired.

If a man can play NFL football at the age of forty-eight, there is no excuse to not do something because you are too old. No Super Bowl was ever won with rookies. Every season that a player plays they get better and better, and if they don't, it has to do with something interfering with their thoughts about themselves, the game, or any other distraction that they allow to take over their focus. The experiences of the previous season can be learned from, and adjusted to, in order to create a new successful season. The experience of vetted players assists in the development of rookies on the field and encourages new players to play their best game. Here again we focus on the fact that winning at anything in life is 90 percent mental and 10 percent physical.

You're never too old to play in the game of life. Your earlier experiences create the trajectory for your next chapter. And the older you get, the better you are at being You. That being said, how do you know when it's time to be traded, quit a team, change players on your roster, or even change the game you're playing? Answer: *when it stops working.* When you feel you don't want to get up in the morning. You're bored, resentful, fatigued, angry, or just plain ... disappointed in life. Regardless of what gets you there, you'll know when you arrive, and if you turn inward for assistance, you will wake up one day and know exactly what you need to do, just like I did, at whatever age it happens to be.

Core Belief: You Are Never Too Old to Accomplish Anything

Wow, this one is important. Our society is so focused on the power of youth that we seem to have forgotten the power of experience and knowledge. Did you know that our frontal lobes, which are responsible for our ability to make decisions, aren't even fully developed until we are in our mid-twenties? That's why teenagers are so impulsive. It also means that, by the time we're thirty, we're just getting the hang of making well-informed decisions. So that would also mean, in our forties, we're finally really good at predicting outcomes and developing well-planned strategies, and in our fifties, we're now pros. In our sixties, good decisions are second nature, and in our seventies and eighties, we can see how foolish youth can be, and we know why: that lack of a fully functioning brain and a minimum of experience. So, too old? No way! Actually, life experience is your best friend.

What are your assumptions about how you should be living at your age? Do some work for you, and if so, which ones? What would you be doing differently if age weren't a consideration? Are any of the assumptions about what's age-appropriate for you accurate? If so, how can you make a plan that takes them into consideration while still living your dream? If not, why are you so afraid?

Game On!

Chapter Six

The Monkette

-6-

I planned and saved, and finally, in 2006, it was time to make the move. Noelle had already moved to California almost a year before me. I thought it would be a great experiment if she went first because if it didn't work out with her, I could bring her back, put her in therapy, and cancel the whole idea. She didn't think I was funny. Off she went anyway, her brother Jonathan following a few months later. And although I was overjoyed that Noelle and Jonathan would be in California with me, my son Jason pulled at my heartstrings by remaining in New York.

Buzz and I packed up our belongings, and before I knew it, my driver's license read that I was a California resident. After settling in, Buzz flew back to New York to stay at the apartment we'd kept in Manhattan and return to work. For the next few years, we maintained a long-distance relationship, and our marriage was better than it'd been in years. With him flying in for long weekends, we found new excitement and passion.

I was mostly committed to freeing myself of my past. Our new home was bigger and more beautiful than any we'd ever owned before, and it was on the side of a mountain in a gated community. This was the moment when I finally practiced what I'd long been preaching and made the space to *breathe*. I left my fast-paced life and became a monkette.

For the first time in years, I was at leisure to walk my dog. Walking my dog in the mountains of southern California was an amazing experience for me, kind of like when an NFL rookie takes to the stadium field for the first time. There's so much to take in: the size of the stadium, the number of fans, and the loudness of sounds bouncing off the stadium walls. They experience the feeling of their physicality and how it compares to their new surrounding environment, which was sort of what I felt as I walked on the mountain paths and realized that the twigs in front of me were moving. Why? Because they weren't twigs, they were f****** snakes! What does a New Yorker do when she realizes she's in the path of snakes? Yes, that's right—she screams like a little girl and starts running. And she learns to bring a stick with her the next time she goes on a hike. Me? I learned, you don't need to go hiking in the mountains; walking around the block will do just fine. (But you can be sure I took that stick anyway.) Still, nature was intriguing to me. I started to accept the snakes and the coyotes. Oh and by the way, coyotes like to eat small dogs. My dog, Nikki, was a seven-pound Maltese. Needless to say, she stayed close to me. I'm used to rats in the subway system that stay to themselves, hoping you'll drop your food when you see them. Seeing wildlife that's looking at you as food was all new to me. But the silver lining was that there was a vibration in California that I seemed to connect with. I vibrated better there and I didn't know why.

I learned how to slow down and enjoy life, and through this process, I came to really appreciate nature. I literally saw flowers and birds for what felt like was the first time ever. One of the very first days I was in my new home, after I had put the last packing box away, I stood on my deck with a cup of coffee, took a deep breath, and marveled at the beautiful view off my balcony. Suddenly, something flew before me and hovered only two feet in front of my face. It took me a moment to realize it was a hummingbird. It seemed to be as curious about me as I was of it. We stood there for a few moments staring at each other, and I laughed. "Oh you're a hummingbird!" I said out loud. "It's so nice to meet you." And that's how I felt. It was so nice to meet "life." As it should be. Free and happy. Wildlife is not concerned with making money. Wildlife exists in the present, eating only what it needs for that day, knowing that there will be a place to sleep that night, and curious of all that surrounds them. Humans, on the other hand, either live in the past or the future, never really taking a moment to breathe and appreciate the "day." I made a commitment right then to change that.

As I took walks around my new community, I looked at the trees and noticed the leaves. I'd always known trees had leaves, but I'd never stopped to look at them. My life had always moved so fast that I'd never appreciated its wonders. *I've been missing this world because I was working so much in it*, I thought. I remembered my mom acknowledging how hard I was working and the little time I had for myself as she said, "My darling daughter, you might want to stop for a minute and smell the roses before it's too late." I brushed her off at the time, but I was beginning to realize just how important her words were.

My mom wasn't the only one who'd seen it. I had a boss who'd once looked at me and asked a hard question.

"Are you running away from something, or are you running toward something?" he asked. "Because you're definitely running."

Even at that time I knew he was right. I was running and I'd always been running. For some reason, I'd always thought I was going to die young, and so I'd been in a hurry to do everything—to get married, have a family, and launch my career. And for all of these years, he was the only one who'd seen it because the way I'd operated my life had worked for everyone else. I was a wife and mother and had been taking care of a family, as I should, and so they'd never thought to question how I was living or if it worked for me. Only now, I hadn't died young, and I didn't have anyone to take care of, except for myself. Maybe I'd been running when I moved to California, but it was then that I realized I wasn't running away from something; I was running toward something, and now I was where I was supposed to be.

I know all of this sounds like a fairy tale, and up to this point it felt like one ... until the fear of it all started rushing in. The self-doubt started tapping me on the shoulder. The house was empty. There was no one to talk to. Oops! Life as I knew it had come to a screeching halt, and it felt like I was just about to hit a brick wall. Then the negative thoughts started. *What have I done?*

One morning, when Buzz was in New York and my kids were living their new lives and I didn't have anywhere I needed to be, I was still in bed at eleven o'clock. I didn't want to get up. I couldn't get up. I pulled the covers over my head. And then it hit me: *Oh no, I know what this is. This is depression, and I'm not doing it.* I threw back the covers and leapt out of bed. Even though I didn't feel like it, I made myself get dressed, put on my stilettos, and go out into the world. I knew I had to change my thoughts, and do it fast.

I'd always had a saying when my kids or clients were crying: "Okay, you get fifteen minutes to feel sorry for yourself." I would look at my watch as I timed them. It might seem cold, but it always got them to laugh at themselves and the situation that was getting them down.

Clearly, we have to feel emotions and let them work through our bodies, but then, it's time to look at them and make a plan for how to move forward. I'd given myself my fifteen minutes, and now I was ready to move forward. But how? Well, first things first ... my Starbucks. Yes, every new adventure in my life starts with Starbucks, so off I went. Once inside, I ordered my drink, and the barista asked me how my day was going.

"Not so good," I replied.

"Well then, this coffee is on the house," he said with a big smile.

"No, you don't have to do that."

"No, I don't, but I will," he insisted.

And then it dawned on me how I could never allow anyone to give me something for free. I decided to make a change that moment.

"Okay, that's very nice of you."

I had changed my thoughts. I was going to let someone give me something without having to reciprocate. I was changing my thoughts and allowing myself to receive. It was a struggle, but I held fast and took the coffee, thanking him. I have to admit I did say thank you more times than necessary, felt a little foolish, and thought *this is going to take some getting used to.* At that moment, something made me look down at an open newspaper, and I read, "The latest and greatest new book, *The Secret.*" With Barnes & Noble right next door, I decided that a good book might just do the trick. I went in to buy it, but they were sold out. The cashier told me that they couldn't keep it on the shelves. So of course, I had to order it, and a few days later I was reading a book that would change my life—or I should say I was reading another book that charted the course for where I am today. This book sits on my nightstand today, symbolizing for me that defining moment of my life that gave me direction and an understanding of what I've been experiencing my whole life; I just never had a name for it.

Rhonda Byrne's book, *The Secret*, had to do with the Law of Attraction and how we are all connected. I always knew there was an invisible force playing in my life, but I didn't understand how or why. Like that time my girlfriend Denise called me at home and insisted I meet her at a bar. Her husband had died suddenly at an early age, and she was left with three young children. Every day seemed like a struggle for her, and I tried to support her the best I could. I didn't want to go out that night but something was insisting that I go. At first, I thought I was feeling guilty because she had to go out by herself, but I would shortly realize it was more than that. I begrudgingly showed up, and there was Denise talking to four men. As I approached, we all sat down at a table and started introducing ourselves. When it was my turn, I stated that I was a substance-abuse counselor. Interesting, yes, that out of all the jobs I had that was the one that came out of my mouth? The table went silent and it got a little weird. I asked what was wrong.

The guy sitting next to me volunteered, "These guys just broke me out of rehab. I'm an alcoholic." And he put down his scotch.

There it was. I knew why I was there. "That's a tough journey. I guess it hasn't been going well," I said.

As he held his scotch and swirled it in the glass, I continued, "You know, you have a choice, and each carries consequences. If you want, you could go back to rehab right now and start over tomorrow, or drink that scotch and live with the consequences that brought you to rehab in the first place."

There was a moment of silence because we all knew this was a defining moment for him. He smelt his drink, thought about it for a moment, and then laid it to rest on the table. He stood up and told his buddies he was ready to leave. He bent down, and I thought he was going to kiss me good-bye. Instead, he whispered in my ear, "Thank you. I needed to run into you tonight."

I never saw that man again, and if I bumped into him today, I wouldn't even recognize him. There are no chance meetings. We are all in this game of life together, and the bigger picture is that we are all on the same team, just trying to get through our own tournament with the least injuries.

The Law of Attraction is the name given to the belief that "like attracts like." It contends that whatever you focus on will manifest, whether it be positive or negative. I spent the next year studying quantum physics and how energy works, along with the Law of Attraction and its relationship to positive manifestation. This led me to study the power of meditation and visualization and how everything is connected as people and their thoughts are both made from pure energy.

I opened up a small private practice and had my clients learn to meditate and work with the Law of Attraction in their lives. The results were amazing. I wanted to reach more people, so I developed a website, HeartCockles.com, where I could sell heart cockleshells with a written scroll instructing people on how to meditate and visualize.

There's even a behind-the-scenes story on how I stumbled upon the heart cockleshells that I began importing from the Philippines. Noelle wasn't having much luck on the dating scene, to the point that she didn't even want to go out on dates anymore. I felt she was spending way too much time at home and became concerned. At the same time, I had gone to San Diego for a weekend getaway, and as I was shopping in the local stores, I came across an adorable pink and white cockleshell that was in the shape of a heart. I bought it, thinking of her. When I got home, I put it in a box and made up a story. I knew that if she visualized and meditated on being in a happy, healthy relationship, according to the Law of Attraction, it would eventually manifest. So my story went like this:

"Noelle, the lady at the store told me that this heart cockleshell was a special shell from the Philippines. If you hold it in your hand and visualize your perfect partner and feel how happy you will be when he arrives, he will appear."

She responded, "Yeah right, Mom."

"Your energy will go out to him through your meditation, and he will find you. You need to do this every night for thirty days. Believe it will happen, and it will."

She rolled her eyes at me, as she often did.

That didn't stop me. "Okay, it's your choice. Either you'll make it happen or you won't. But I'll tell you one thing: you keep rolling your eyes like that and they're going to get stuck in the top of your head and you won't get any dates for sure!"

And then it dawned on me. I could put together a website and sell these heart cockles as focusing tools along with scrolls teaching people how to meditate, change their thoughts, and use the Law of Attraction to manifest their dreams. Game on!

Three months later Heartcockles.com was launched. My reading about quantum physics and my appreciation for the small details and moments in nature and life were teaching me about all that's not tangible. Although I had always felt that there was something beyond our visible existence, I began to understand what it was. We can't see it, but we can feel it, and it felt great. I was so moved by what I was learning that I took everything I knew about positive thinking, the Law of Attraction, meditation, and visualization and packaged it so that others could join my journey. And, just like that, many did.

Even though nothing had happened with the show at this point, I believed with all my being that things were happening behind the scenes. I was resting in California. I was cocooning. For what, I didn't know, but it was already having a positive impact. The twitch I had in my eye and the cyst on my ovary had both gone away on their own. And, inexplicably, the heart murmur I'd been born with had also disappeared. I don't know how that even happens. But, clearly, California was where I was meant to be. I'd changed my thoughts, I'd changed my life, and I knew my success would come. A very important lesson that I'd come to know at this juncture was that the moment you get off the "gimme" lane and get on the "thank-you" lane many wonderful things begin to happen. It's positive energy attracting positive energy.

You know what happens before something big happens? Nothing! "No-thing" happens, at least on the physical plane. But on the metaphysical plane a lot is happening. Just like that athlete who goes into the zone and connects with what's happening on the field, in life there is the "zone of happening," where things are created from the thoughts generated by your desire. I knew I needed to "allow" things to line up. You need to be where you are in order to get where you're going. But what do you do while "no-thing" is happening? How do you not give up or fall prey to the negativity? Answer: *you refocus the energy you're putting into waiting and create something you can give to others, or yourself.* In my case, I refocused the energy into creating HeartCockles.com. I was helping others as well as myself. I got on the board of our gated community. I made friends. I built a life, and it was one that I, surprisingly, really enjoyed.

Because my daily routine had always been filled with so many people, being alone at my new house in California began to feel like a sanctuary to me the moment I allowed myself to relax in it. For the first time in thirty years, I didn't have anyone in my face, asking me for help or pulling on me, and it felt amazing. Don't get me wrong—I loved my family, but I was tired of being a caretaker. The kids were all grown and healthy and beginning their life's journeys. And for Buzz, I felt I had given all I could and I didn't owe him anything. I was a good wife. I took care of our family for thirty years, kept his homes well cared for, paid for myself to finish school, made good money and contributed financially to household bills and luxuries, and did my wifely duties happily. This was my turn, and I was going to take it.

Every evening, I went out onto my balcony and felt grateful. The view was breathtaking as I overlooked the city of Ontario and beyond. All I saw from my mountaintop were the twinkling red and green traffic lights as they flashed on the freeways at dusk, and the lights from the thousands of homes below me. It looked like Christmas every night of the year. I looked up to the sky. "Thank you," I said. And I said it every night.

Core Belief: Be Grateful for Where You Are in Life; You're Exactly Where You Need to Be

Looking back, I can see that, if I hadn't gone through each and every hardship—as well as the good times—I couldn't have achieved my goals. And so, at this point in my life, no matter where I am on my path, I take every opportunity to thank the heavens for my good fortune. When hard times present themselves, I look for the lesson in the experience. I ask myself, "What am I learning right now?" And lo and behold, my next thought contains the answer, and I am able to become grateful. There truly is a silver lining in every disappointment. Find them, and even the events that don't seem ideal will become moments you can learn from and find a way to cherish.

How has the path through which you achieved a goal actually made you more able to enjoy that accomplishment to the fullest? Can you think of an occurrence that seemed like a setback at the time but was actually an important part of your personal growth, or even a positive, in the long run? What do you have to be grateful for *right now*? What are you currently struggling with that is teaching you something you can use in the future?

Chapter Seven

It's Not Over Yet

-7-

After my initial honeymoon period with California and the new state of my life and my marriage, everything seemed to hit a rocky patch. The economy tanked, and Buzz started to lose business and investments. I was hitting my savings and watching the numbers in my checkbook dwindle down.

During this whole time, I trusted that I was meant to have this space for myself, even though it was the result of the fact that we hadn't sold the show yet, no matter that my brother and I had redoubled our efforts. Two years into my new life in California, which was five years into our pitching efforts and never letting anyone's *no* be the end of our dream, we'd come very close, but it still hadn't happened.

It was taking longer than I'd thought it would. For a moment, I doubted. It crossed my mind that maybe I should get a job in the local school district, just until the show happened. The thought literally made me want to throw up. That was exactly the course correction I'd needed, the reminder that I was where I needed to be. Not long after that, Buzz was in California while Noelle was over, and he brought up the possibility that maybe I should turn back.

"Maybe you should come back to New York," he said.

Tears instantly started pouring out of my eyes, but I didn't feel like I was crying.

"I know you see me crying," I said. "I'm not really crying. I think my body is crying. I'm having the weirdest feeling right now."

"What?!" Noelle said. "What does that even mean?"

The thought of going back was so horrible to me that it literally made my body cry. To this day, I'm not even sure what was physically happening, but many times during the trials and tribulations of my life, my body has taken over and reacted in such a way that it told me the real truth I needed to know. As it happened, I felt moved to make this statement, not even understanding what it meant: "Every cell of my body is telling me to stay exactly where I am."

It felt very similar to what happened at my first administrative job in Commack Middle School. I had been there four years. It was the end of the school year, I had packed up my office to go on summer vacation, and as I was walking my boxes out to my car, I turned to look at the school now behind me. As I did, I felt with every cell of my body that I wouldn't be coming back next year. I didn't know why—I wasn't looking for another job. Where this feeling came from, I didn't know. A few weeks into my vacation I got a call that a school district in Nassau County was opening a new position for an administrator of counseling services, and they wanted me to apply. I did. I got the job, and that fall I was in a new school, in a bigger position making more money. I was there for a few months, and the same thing happened again. I was driving to work one morning, and I got the feeling that next year I wouldn't be there. I knew full well that jumping from school district to school district wasn't a good thing, but every cell of my body told me that I would be. I chuckled, thinking, *I've felt this before. I guess I'll just wait and see what happens.* At the end of that school year, they released me as they were closing the position. This happened several times more in my career, and every time it happened, my next position was bigger, better, and provided a higher salary. And yet, at this junction of trying to sell the show, I still doubted. I became afraid.

FEAR is False Evidence Appearing Real and truly is a complicated emotion. We have been genetically programmed to respond to it. Its initial intention was to keep us safe. Back in the caveman days we counted on it as dinosaurs saw us as food. It caused us to either fight or take flight. But today, the "dinosaur" we fear is failure. And failure, to some people, will eat them alive.

Fear is another word for *don't*, and the word *don't* stops most of us in our tracks. It causes us to doubt, have negative thoughts, and more tragically, not trust our inner voice, which ultimately paralyzes our forward movement in life. Fear originates in childhood when our parents felt it their duty to pass on their fears as they worked diligently until they made us fear the things they feared. Although well-meaning, they handed down their irrational fears. Ultimately, we develop tapes in our subconscious that dictate behavior, and that behavior translates into "playing it safe," "not stepping out of the box," and "being afraid of failure," rather than "no pain, no gain," "take the road less traveled," and "the bigger the risk, the better the payoff." All people who are successful in life take gambles, they never doubt, they never quit, they never let anyone get in their way, and they ultimately never lose. My entire life has been one gamble after another, but it's the waiting period that destroys our confidence, and for me, it was really twisting me up.

And then one day I took hold of myself and asked, "What would I do if I weren't afraid?" That was the question I had asked myself when I looked up the NY Jets trainer's number and hesitated the moment before I made the call. If I weren't afraid, I would just do it and whatever happened, happened. But actually, with that call I did one more thing. Before I made the call, I sat still, closed my eyes, took a deep breath, and visualized the way I wanted the call to go. I visualized him picking up the phone and speaking with me. And that's exactly what happened. Most people would have been afraid to make that call, so why wasn't I? Because I chose not to be. I believe there are no mistakes in life, just choices and consequences. I chose to succeed, and in order to do that I had to make that call. So I did. But not before I visualized how I wanted it to go and held on to the feeling of how great it would be when I had accomplished my goal.

I realized at that moment that I was at the same place as I was when I was calling the trainer every two weeks—and was made to wait. I needed to be patient then, and I needed to be patient now. The problem? I was never good at waiting. I don't know about you, but waiting for something to happen while nothing is happening feels like falling into a void. Having come this far, though, and having studied quantum physics and the Law of Attraction, I knew what I had to do.

I needed to take that void and embrace it. I needed to believe that the universe was orchestrating everything perfectly behind the scenes. I needed to meditate and visualize my TV show in all its magnificence and prepare for when it eventually happened. I began to focus on the positive, not on delays and disappointment. I focused on what was working in my life and all I had to be grateful for. When fearful thoughts snuck in, I turned them around with grateful thoughts, knowing that grateful thoughts were positive thoughts on steroids.

When Buzz came to me and said he couldn't do it anymore, I responded, "I couldn't *not* do it." And then I did what athletes do: I dug in and hoped for a "Hail Mary." Sometimes the best play is the one that's not in the book. You've heard of the "Hail Mary" in football. Well, the game of life is filled with them. They're the last-minute actions that you take when everything seems to be falling apart, and somehow it's that play that saves the day. Yes, we all want a win, and many times it's not until the last minute that everything seems to line up perfectly. Hanging in till that part, my friends, is the hardest thing to do. It separates the winners from the losers. It's when we go to our core and make that final decision to fight to the end. It's having faith in the fact that there is sense to all of this that we call "life," and we won't understand it until we are at the close of our life and we get to reflect.

It was in this moment of my new life in California, when every cell of my body was screaming, "You can't turn back now!" that I listened. I stayed. I toughed it out. I continued to focus on the positive I was creating, rather than the delays and disappointments.

Joe and I had started working with a new writer, and the three of us began going to pitch meetings together. We received interest from Warner Brothers. This was exciting, but we'd received interest many times before, and it had never come to anything, so I kept my expectations in check. And then, Warner Brothers picked up the show. But when the deal was on the table, the writer insisted on a pay-or-play deal, meaning he'd get paid even if the show didn't get made. Warner Brothers refused. We had a meeting with our writer to try to change his mind.

"We can't believe you're doing this," I said.

"My advisors told me to do it," he said. "And I'm going to follow my advisors."

Joe and I looked at each other. *What are we going to say to that?*

All we could do was hope that Warner Brothers could be convinced to see it his way. Soon after that, Joe showed up at my house one evening. He lived in Sherman Oaks, and it was a big deal for him to drive an hour east to my place in Rancho Cucamonga. When I answered the doorbell, I couldn't believe he was really standing there.

"What are you doing here?" I said.

"I've got something to tell you," he replied. *Something happened to our parents,* I thought, already fearing the worst.

"What?"

"Warner Brothers passed."

"Oh, that's it? I thought somebody died. You scared the hell out of me!"

"I didn't want to tell you on the phone. I didn't know what you'd do."

"What did you think I was going to do? We'll just keep going. Somebody else will pick it up. Warner Brothers wanted it. Someone else will want it. It's a good thing."

As I washed the dishes that night, every cell of my body was telling me we needed to take it to a cable network. I smiled to myself, thinking, *I don't know how that's going to happen, but you haven't been wrong before. It wouldn't surprise me if that's where it winds up.*

We need to train ourselves to listen to our instincts. I'm not a psychic, but the reality is that we all have an inner voice, our intuition. And I'm sure many of you can attest to the fact that when you don't follow your gut, things go wrong. At this point I had learned to listen to my inner voice, to get out of its way and "allow."

That's how I really felt with the news from Warner Brothers. Was I disappointed? Yes, but I knew if we could get to the point where we could sell it to Warner Brothers, we could sell it to somebody else. And WB's *no* wasn't any more meaningful than any other *no* we'd gotten over the years. I chose to be patient, believing that everything happens for a reason.

So the deal disappeared, and we parted ways with that writer. Joe and I were back at square one ... where we'd started out in the beginning, only we'd learned so much during the six years so far. And I was still determined that I was going to make the show happen somehow. But then, in November 2007, the writers went on strike. Nothing would happen now for sure. When the strike ended the following February and the writers went back to work, most of the pending deals that had been picked up before the strike were all thrown away. So if we had signed with Warner Brothers, we might have lost everything anyhow. See? Everything happens for a reason, and we were exactly where we were supposed to be, even if it didn't really feel like it. At least we could still keep pitching our show. As I've said, you can't know the significance of an event until after the fact. Everything works out in the end, and if it hasn't worked out, it's just not the end yet. We kept going. In fact, we were even more determined.

When I was ready to walk away, which I was on several occasions, Joe wasn't ready to walk away. And then something would happen to keep the show moving, even just a little bit further, toward our goal. When Joe was ready to walk away, I wasn't ready to walk away, and again, something positive would happen. Talk about a good team. Whether it was a meeting, somebody offering to help us, or even just an encouraging e-mail, something always kept us in the game.

Many people have asked me why I didn't quit during those long and winding seven years. Well, there was always something positive to keep me going. *The Secret* tells us that if we visualize what we want, it will manifest. To a point, that's true, but we need to do something to move the energy forward, even if it's one small task every day. If you want to be a doctor, you can't just sit on the couch and visualize yourself in surgery without physically attending medical school, so you do need to "do" something. And that's what Joe and I kept doing. We kept networking, talking to whomever we could, keeping our vision alive, and believing success was just around the corner.

Sometimes getting frustrated and feeling like I'd done all I could do was actually the best thing that could happen to me. When I gave up trying for a bit, that moment of surrender often led the universe to gift us something, moving us closer to our goal. It wasn't over yet, and I knew it.

Core Belief: Be Patient, Knowing That Everything Happens for a Reason

It's always important to remember that we don't know what's going to happen next, or how a particular relationship or event in our life is going to play out. What seems like a disappointment or a setback today often turns out to be a positive in the long run. The story of our stymied Warner Brothers deal is the perfect example of this. Yes, it turned out better in the long run that the deal didn't go through except that I didn't know any of that in the moment. Luckily, I trusted that I would find another way to reach my goal, and I did. It's all about maintaining a flexible perspective and a positive outlook.

Now it's your turn. When did something in your life seem to have a negative outcome that turned out to be a positive? What is one area of your life where you could be more patient? How can you practice greater patience? What can you learn from a setback you've recently experienced? Can you turn this setback into a positive?

Game On!

Chapter Eight

All It Takes Is One

Yes

-8-

After Warner Brothers picked us up and then let us go, I knew what I had to do ... find another writer. The exec at WB was a champion of my story and worked with me to find a new writer. It takes only one *yes* to move forward, and I was determined to find it. I needed a new team, and it was becoming more and more frustrating as each of the writers she recommended was already committed to another project. After we'd come so close, it suddenly felt like we couldn't get anywhere at all.

But I held fast. I needed inspiration, and one day it was sent to me. As I opened my e-mails one morning, one in particular caught my attention, TUT.com. This website was co-founded by Mike Dooley and is a web-based inspirational and philosophical Adventurers Club. I subscribed to his free *Notes from the Universe*, where every morning I received an inspirational note. It was one of those things that seemed to speak to you when you read it. It helped me. Many mornings it was just the thing I needed to keep me moving in a positive direction. To this day, I read them every morning.

This was about the same time that I wanted to start the Heart Cockles website, but I wasn't computer savvy and didn't have the slightest idea how to start one. It just so happened that I had received a jury duty notice and was required to be in court the following week. I tried to get out of it but couldn't. So I took some reading material and headed off to my appointed courthouse. As I walked in, there was only one seat left. I sat down next to a woman, and we exchanged pleasantries and began talking. One thing led to another, and she told me she ran a computer company that develops and hosts websites. Really?! Needless to say, she got a client and we became friends. Gale's company, developed and hosts HeartCockles.com. She was now a part of my Heart Cockles team. But I needed more teammates. I needed someone who was good at searching the Internet for the cockleshells and the materials needed to make the product. My daughter-in-law Janell fit the bill and wanted to be part of it, along with Noelle who would be in charge of shipping and customer relations. Opening an S-Corp was no big deal; Legal Zoom made it easy. It's all about finding the team that believes in your dream. There was my team!

Okay, that was done, but I was still in the void. There was no movement with regard to the show. Joe and

I were still trying everything we could, but we had a lot of down time. Again, the void could last a long time, but if you keep creating and putting out positive energy, things will manifest. That's what the Law of Attraction tells us. That's what meditation and visualization tells us. Yet, I still had nothing.

One day Joe was making fun of how difficult it was for me to learn the game of football.

I said to him, "Really, why is a goal worth six points? Why isn't it one point or three? Why six? There's no rhyme or reason to it."

"It's easy to remember," he said.

"Yeah, if you're a guy."

He shook his head. "Why is that?"

"'Cause the game was developed by men and *six* sounds like *sex*, so that makes sense to guys." I chuckled.

Then we both looked at each other and agreed that we should write a book explaining the game of football to women. We all have memory hooks, and relationships are important to women, so if we explain football using relationship memory hooks, it will be easier for them to understand and remember the rules of the game and be able to talk to their weekend warrior partners about it. We can make fun of men and their fascination with the game and associate football with relationships. It will be funny, informative, and educational all at the same time.

Three months later, our book, *A Woman's Guide to the Knuckledragging Sport of Football*, was written.

In addition to being an actor, Joe manages an apartment building, and around this time, a woman, Marley, came to look at an apartment for her parents because she was trying to convince them to move to Los Angeles. She told Joe that her last name was Dowling.

"I know a Kevin Dowling," Joe said. "He was the director on a show I did."

"Oh, Kevin's my husband," she said.

So Joe pitched her our show.

"Wow, that sounds really interesting," Marley continued. "I should tell Kevin."

She went home that night and told Kevin about our show.

"Everybody has a pitch," Kevin said.

She knew this was true, but she really believed it was a good idea, and she kept pushing him. (She's a woman after my own heart, and she never let the word *no* stop her either.) Finally, Kevin called me. By this point, I was talking to another writer, so I pushed Kevin off. A few weeks went by, nothing was working out, calls between Kevin and myself went back and forth, and I eventually agreed to meet with him. As soon as I did, I immediately believed he could make this happen.

Much of what goes into picking a team is instinctual. When we meet someone who's going to be a true ally, we can often sense the positive connection right off the bat. The best thing we can do, always, is to trust our inner voice. Once we'd decided on Kevin, he lined up a couple of writers for us to interview, and as soon as we met Liz Kruger and Craig Shapiro, we fell in love with them. Together, we formed a collective to pitch the show. And after all of that, Marley's parents never moved to California. But if Kevin's wife hadn't gone to look at that apartment, we might never have made that connection with them in the first place. There's that invisible force again, working behind the scenes. The universe is pretty amazing, am I right?

By this point, when we went into meetings, I had my pitch down cold: "This show is about a female therapist working with high-profile athletes, CEOs, and politicians. She's a girly girl in a man's world." From there, I told them my life story, how I didn't know anything about sports, and some of the funniest anecdotes from my time with the Jets.

For example, the players would often take their sweet time getting to their appointments with me. I always had a tight schedule, so if any of them ran late, their appointment would run into the next appointment, so I figured out a way to put a stop to that. Anyone who was late needed to bring me my Starbucks coffee of choice to their next appointment, and if they were late for that one, they would either have to take Nikki (my seven-pound Maltese) to the groomer or pick her up at the next visit. This actually started out as a joke, but for some reason they all thought I was serious, and so I found many cups of coffee at my sessions, and I had the cleanest dog on the block. Now that I think about it, I think they enjoyed it. It made them feel connected.

It was always interesting how they connected to my family and took an interest in what was happening with us. One evening, a player was waiting for his appointment in my family room when the doorbell rang. He took it upon himself to answer it, and when he opened the door, there stood an African American friend of Noelle. The player (African American himself) told the kid she wasn't home, which she was, and when he came into my office for his appointment, he said, "What's Noelle doin' with a brother?" I got the feeling it was a rhetorically disapproving comment. I laughed. He was married to a white woman.

My son Jonathan, who had joined the school football team, asked one of my linebacker clients for some tips on certain plays. When the player came into his session, he told me that my son had accosted him outside the office. I apologized. He responded, "White boys shouldn't play football. He's goin' to get hurt." I laughed as he limped into my office, took a seat, and turned up his electronic muscle-stimulating device that was attached to his knee.

Even my mom had dealings with them. She would come over to our house as she lived only fifteen minutes away. In the evening she would be checking up on the kids, especially when Buzz was on the road and she knew I was seeing clients. This one night she was attempting to go up my driveway in her red Pinto as a player was attempting to go down my driveway in his yellow Lamborghini. Only one car could fit, and my mom thought it should be hers. He thought it should be his. So my mom began to rev her engine, and then, of course, the player revved his. And then the scream from Noelle, "Mom, Grandma is having a standoff with your client!"

What?! I ran outside and assessed the situation. I went to the player and told him it was my mom and he better back up—I'd experienced her back swing. He sighed, "Sounds like my mom," he said as he put his car in reverse.

There was also the player who complained, "The NFL owns you, man. They tell you what you can and cannot do. They weigh you, measure you, and then fine you if you are not within the specifications that they determine makes for the best player. The white man is still holding me down."

"You get paid millions of dollars, and you really feel that the white man is holding you down?!" I retorted. "Is that what you think of me?"

"NO, you're my dog," he replied.

"Your dog?! What the hell kind of a comment is that?" I questioned.

"It means you're special to me."

"You mean, I'm like your wingman?"

"What the hell does that mean?" he asked.

Lost in translation for sure. But the feelings were genuine, caring, and important, and the TV execs knew it. You couldn't make this stuff up.

When I gave my pitch to Sharon Hall from SONY, she loved it. She signed us and brought us to USA Network, a cable network. I found it interesting that I had felt instinctively that cable was where the show belonged.

"If those writers can get on the page what Donna just told us, we have a hit show," the executive at USA said.

So USA picked up the show, and then it was up to the writers. Now we had to deliver a script, and it was anything but a seamless process. The first script came across to me.

"What do you think?" Liz said.

"Well, do you want me to be honest?" I said.

"Yeah."

"You just put everything in there that I told you," I said. "You didn't create anything."

Even though we weren't exactly off to the strongest start, I didn't let it worry me, and I never doubted my team. Much of life—particularly the creative life—is a matter of trial and error. I knew they were the best writers for the project and the best teammates for me, so I was honest about my expectations, and then I stepped back and let her do her job.

She took the script and reworked it, and when she sent it back to me, she'd pumped it up a lot. I was over-the-top excited to finally get to the next step.

"I like that," I said. "I like that a lot!"

But there was one aspect of the pilot that gave me pause, and it ended up being a *big* conversation amongst our creative team. They had written (spoiler alert!) that the character based on me separates from her husband, and she goes out with her girlfriend and sleeps with the team's athletic trainer, basically implying that I slept my way into the NFL. I had a problem with that because I did not sleep my way into the NFL by any stretch of the imagination. We went back and forth, and back and forth.

"You're basing this on my life," I said, "and that's a big issue. I don't like the message that it sends, and it's not the truth."

They told me it wasn't a documentary, and it wasn't going to be a 100 percent accurate. They felt that, if she was a single woman, it gave them more room to explore her character than if she was married. I was so conflicted that I went out to a lot of people, men and women, and I asked them the same question.

"If you saw a show about this, and the woman slept with this guy, and so it's implied that she sleeps her way into the NFL, would you respect her character?"

It was a fifty-fifty split between both men and women; half said they didn't like it, and the other half said they did. There were even some women that said, "I have no problem with it. That's exactly what I did."

So I went back and told everyone what I'd learned, but I still couldn't let go of how bothered I was. Finally, Kevin, our director who was also an executive producer, told me that we had to go with this storyline because it was more interesting, and that I could then go and do interviews and tell everybody that was the part of the show that wasn't real.

I didn't honestly feel like I had a choice if I wanted the show to get made, and I trusted them. They were my team. I knew they believed in me and wanted me to succeed and that this belief had to go both ways, so I agreed. We turned the script in to the USA network, and they gave us the green light to shoot the pilot. Even with all the obstacles we'd encountered over the years, I'd stayed true to my core beliefs and never lost sight of who I was, or what I knew I could do. And now, it was really happening. Seven years after my brother and I had first begun pitching the show, we had actually sold it. We flew to Atlanta in 2010 to shoot the pilot.

We were scheduled to be in Atlanta for forty-two days. When we checked into our hotel rooms, the clerk asked Joe and me how many room keys we wanted.

"One," Joe said.

"Two," I said. My brother looked over at me, surprised. "If I'm going to be here for forty-two days, I'm making friends," I said.

He laughed, and I laughed, too. But I was serious. I had set myself free, and I was going to experience that freedom to the utmost and never stop. I was never going to let anyone define what that should look like. It's really hard to leave the known world for a dream that may not come true, but the rewards are infinite and just keep growing.

Well, just because you make a pilot doesn't mean you have a TV series. That pilot has to go to the execs at SONY and USA for their approval, then out to the public to be tested. Then and only then, after jumping through many hoops, does it get green lit. Many pilots are produced each year, and only about 1 to 2 percent of those shot make it on the screen. But we fell into that 1 percent, and in December of 2010, *Necessary Roughness*'s writers' office opened up in Burbank, California, with its filming offices and crew settling in Atlanta.

Joe and I now needed to meet with the writing team; the first one was our show runner, Jeffrey Lieber. When we met him for lunch, he asked me to tell him about our journey, so I did, emphasizing that Joe and I did this without an agent or a manager. He just stared at me. I asked him what he was thinking.

"Do you know what the chances were of you getting this done?" he replied.

"Yes, I've been hearing that it doesn't happen often."

"This doesn't happen at all," he replied.

I told him that I was a proponent of the philosophy that when you want something act "as if" it has already happened, and it will. Even more perplexed, he asked me to explain. I told him that I never doubted the show would get on the air. I even asked Liz where the writers' room would be so that I could move closer to it. She suggested I not do that until it was finalized. I told her I couldn't wait; we'd be shooting soon. I didn't mind her, and I rented an apartment and bought an expensive writer's bag and an awesome keychain to put the office keys on. She chimed in, "Yes, it's bizarre." Maybe so, but there we were, so maybe it wasn't that far-fetched.

Many people have asked me what made me think I could do this, and the only answer I can come up with is that it never dawned on me that I couldn't. Sure, I got frustrated. It did take longer than I had imagined. But really, how hard could it be? I just needed one person to say yes, and I never stopped believing that it would happen.

I knew I couldn't do it by myself; no one achieves anything like this alone. Great players alone don't win Super Bowls; great teams do. The toughest part is picking the players on your team. It's easy after that: they just have to show up, bring their best game every day to work, then turn it over to the universe after collectively visualizing the win. And that's what we wound up doing.

We scored three years of successful shows, along with mental health awards for highlighting mental health awareness. We all had won that proverbial Super Bowl.

Core Belief: You Need People—Pick the Team That Believes in Your Dream

I *really* like this belief because it points to an interesting distinction in the whole process of manifesting your dreams. We might sometimes feel powerless, like we have to do whatever it takes or work with whomever we can, in order to make something happen. This is, and isn't, true. Yes, it's absolutely vital to be flexible, and sometimes we do have to compromise to achieve a goal. But, really, truly, deep down, we pick the people we're meant to grow with at just the time we need them because they're also at exactly the same moment in their lives that they need us, and we can sense this synchronicity in each other. Every person in my life— from my husband, to the administrators and counselors I worked with in the Long Island public school district, to the athletic trainer and players on the Jets during my time there, to the writers on my show—was a huge part of my journey, helping me to become the person I was meant to be. In their own ways, they all believed in me, and I believed in them. I'll always appreciate all of them and the roles they played in helping me to live the best version of my life. I'm continuously building my team as it changes with the different projects I take on to continue my life's journey. It's a huge part of how we grow.

Who's on your team right now? Do they all believe in you and your ability to meet your dreams? If not, is there a way you could get them to become more invested in helping you? Or do you need to consider letting go of a few players on your team and freshening your roster? Who does believe in you? How do they support you, and how can you appreciate this and maximize their support to the fullest? How can you thank your teammates? Always be grateful to these people, the ones who have helped and the ones who have not. They have all served you; they either gave you what you needed, or they strengthened you by not helping you at all.

Game On!

Epilogue

Dreams Do Come

True If You Believe

Epilogue

Whether it be as aggressive as football or as passive as chess, playing in the game of life can be challenging. It takes wit, focus, determination, and perseverance to win the ultimate challenges that life presents. We do have the home-field advantage though, as we are the ones who pick the game, the rules, and the stadium. We get to pick our teams, our uniforms, and our coaches. And then we dare the universe to actually bring us our challenger. And that challenger may come in many forms—as little and as fragile as a newborn baby to as big as Mother Nature's wrath. We strive to succeed, rise above circumstances, and achieve the impossible.

The good news is that in life the cards are actually stacked in our favor. We can all agree that after every storm the waters subside, and the sun does come out again. After every land fire, although the once-beautiful green forest appears to be black and charred, shortly thereafter, as we look closely, we see the sprouting of new life, and before we know it, the forest has been reborn. If we are really honest and stop being dramatic, out of every disappointing event—even loss of life—there is a silver lining. Life has been designed that way to give us hope, second chances, and an opportunity to make the world a better place than we have found it.

As with any sport there are wins and losses, and I will agree that both come with a price. There is a price to pay for greatness as there is a price to pay for quitting. So why play at all? Because we can. Because we're here. Because, quite frankly, what else are we going to do?

Buying that dream house you've always wanted may qualify as winning that Super Bowl. But yes, there is that mortgage payment and we may hold our breath waiting to see if we will have enough money that month for all the bills. Landing that dream job certainly would cause the end-zone dance, yet with every dream job there are aspects of it that we hate. They say football is a game of inches, and often in life it seems that getting to our goals takes so long that we can hardly see any forward motion. In football we get four tries to move the ball ten yards, and the game continues until the clock runs out. Well, in life we have unlimited tries. That clock runs out only at death. We don't have only two hours to play; we have a lifetime. A lifetime of choices and consequences. Of making fumbles or getting touch downs. And through it all we make friends, lovers, families, and sometimes enemies. But in the end the best players walk off the field knowing they did the best they could. And if they were really brave players, they are considered an MVP.

Understanding the psychology behind sports helps us move forward in life. Sports is 90 percent mental and 10 percent physical, as is life. We need to stay physically and mentally healthy. Success begins with eating well, sleeping well, and believing that we can achieve anything we set our minds to. And note: preparation plus opportunity will always equal success ... on the field, and off. Sports teaches us how playing well with others is vital in winning at anything. It shows us that no one succeeds at anything alone. We need people on our team whether they are playing beside us or they are in our corner cheering us on, watering us down during time-outs, or encouraging us to keep practicing every day to become better and better at the game. And at the end of the game, we are lucky if our team is beside us as we walk off the field. It's then that we know we have played well.

As with any doctorate program, mine culminated with a dissertation that had to be defended in front of a group of seasoned doctorial educators. My dissertation was entitled, "Common Elements Among Successful People who Are High School Drop Outs." Quite honestly, it criticized our current educational system in that it doesn't meet the needs of all students. Our society dictates that dropping out of high school is equivalent to signing our lives over to becoming homeless. During my doctorate studies, I was constantly running into people who were highly successful in spite of the fact that they never completed high school. How could that be? Our society indoctrinates us into thinking that it can't be done, yet it's done all the time.

Here again was that invisible force, bringing me to people who were achieving what others said they couldn't. What I found is that there is a common belief system among these people. They all had the belief that they would succeed at anything they wanted in spite of what the educational system was telling them. They were positive thinkers, and their emotional intelligence was very high, meaning they knew how to get along with people and ask for what they needed. They never took *no* for an answer, focused on what they wanted, and never stopped pushing until they got that *yes*. They were amazing networkers as they instinctively knew they couldn't succeed alone. Take a peek at just a few famous high school dropouts:

> **Peter Jennings** – *American television journalist; evening news anchorman*

> **Kemmons Wilson** – *self-made multimillionaire; founder of the Holiday Inn hotel chain*

> **Tommy Lasorda** – *baseball team manager; National Baseball Hall of Fame inductee*

> **Anton van Leeuwenhoek** – *Dutch microscope maker; world's first microbiologist; discoverer of bacteria, blood cells, and sperm cells*

Richard Branson – *self-made billionaire British businessman; founder of Virgin Atlantic Airways and Virgin Records*

Isaac Merrit Singer – *American sewing machine inventor; self-made multimillionaire; founder of Singer Industries (elementary school dropout)*

Charles Chaplin – *Oscar-winning actor, writer, director, producer (elementary school dropout)*

Charles E. Culpeper – *self-made multimillionaire; owner and head of the Coca-Cola Bottling Company*

Marcus Loew – *self-made multimillionaire; founder of Loews movie-theater chain; co-founder of MGM studios (elementary school dropout)*

Mary Lyon – *founder of Mount Holyoke College (America's first women's college)*

Sonny Bono – *singer/songwriter, actor; US congressman (California US representative)*

And just to mention a few of the thousands of actors, writers, singer/songwriters that achieved in a fiercely competitive market and became famous in spite of their lack of a formal education:

Ray Charles, Cher, Pierce Brosnan, Raymond Burr, Glen Campbell, Dizzy Gillespie, Julie Andrews, Louis Armstrong, Pearl Bailey, Lucille Ball, Count Basie, Jack Benny, Humphrey Bogart, Whoopie Goldberg, Danny Thomas, Peter Ustinov, Patrick Stewart, Anthony Quinn, Sophia

Loren, Roy Rogers, Olivia Newton-John, Sydney Poitier, Sean Connery, Joan Crawford, Robert De Niro, Duke Ellington, Ella Fitzgerald, Aretha Franklin, Mark Wahlberg, Charlie Sheen, Christina Applegate, John Travolta, Marlon Brando, Catherine Zeta-Jones, Cameron Diaz, Nicholas Cage, Hilary Swank, Tom Cruise, Quentin Tarantino, Ryan Gosling, Robert Downey Jr., Daniel Radcliffe, Seth Rogen, Jude Law, Nicole Kidman, Al Pacino, Keanu Reeves, Johnny Depp, Bill Cosby, Drew Barrymore, and the list goes on and on.

What about the ordinary people who were not born into success, who started with nothing, overcame unbelievable obstacles, and changed the world? Just to mention a few:

Nelson Mandela, Helen Keller, Rosa Parks, Marie Curie, Beethoven, Florence Nightingale, and Jackie Robinson.

*And who would deny the overwhelming obstacles that **Malala Yousafzai** (born in 1997) faced as a Pakistani schoolgirl who defied threats of the Taliban to campaign for the right to education? She survived being shot in the head by the Taliban and has become a global advocate for human rights, women's rights, and the right to education.*

*Or, **J. K. Rowling**, who inspired a new generation of readers. Newly divorced and struggling to make ends meet, single mom Joanne Rowling turned to work on the novel she had been outlining for five years. Harry Potter and the*

Sorcerer's Stone was published in 1997 under the name "J. K." Rowling because her publisher didn't believe a woman's name would appeal to young boys. Six books and ten years later, Harry Potter has shattered sales records and enthralled millions of readers of all ages.

*And there's **Candy Lightner** who stood up against drunk driving. After her thirteen-year-old daughter was killed by a repeat DWI offender, Candy Lightner founded Mothers Against Drunk Driving (MADD) in her home on March 7, 1980. Before MADD, there were little to no legal consequences for driving while intoxicated; her organization transformed American attitudes about drunk driving and successfully fought for stricter laws across the country.*

Being successful does not require a great deal of skill, talent, or even luck. It doesn't even require hard work. It requires the belief that you can do it. Persistence and dedication to do whatever needs to be done, along with a vision of success, are what turns ordinary people into extraordinary, inspirational motivators.

These two incredibly successful people weren't extraordinary, and they failed many times, but they kept going, in spite of what they were told:

__Dr. Seuss__ is a legendary, world-famous children's author whose books have sold over 600 million copies. However, he didn't start off that way; his first children's book was refused by twenty-seven publishers.

*In 1965, while attending Yale University, **Fred Smith** wrote an economics paper exploring how goods were transported in the United States. Smith thought that a company carrying small, essential items by plane could be a more efficient transporter than existing companies. His professor gave him a "C" for the work. Smith, however, never stopped thinking about creating an express delivery system. He focused and was determined to bring his idea to fruition. In 1982 FedEx introduced the "over-night letter." In 2001, annual FedEx sales reached $20 billion, and the company carries packages to 210 countries.*

Here's just a small sampling of people who quit their jobs and made millions:

Rick Wetzel and Bill Phelps, Wetzel's Pretzels

Rick Wetzel and Bill Phelps were working for Nestle when the concept for Wetzel's Pretzels was born. The two were on a business trip when Wetzel told Phelps about an idea his wife had to make big, soft pretzels to sell at the mall. That night, they sat at a bar and drew out their business plan on a napkin. Wetzel sold his Harley-Davidson to help raise funds for the fledgling business, which they started in their spare time. They brought in a partner to help create the recipe in Phelps' kitchen, and when it came time to open shop, they persuaded a mall landlord to come to the house to try their creation. The landlord liked what he tasted and rented Wetzel's Pretzels its first store.

That was 1994. About a year later, Wetzel and Phelps got their lucky break when they were offered a severance package from Nestle. They opened up several more stores before deciding to franchise in 1996. There are now 250 stores nationwide, with locations set to open in Japan and India. System-wide sales are more than $100 million and same-store sales were up 9 percent in 2011.

Dana Sinkler and Alex Dzieduszycki, Terra Chips

Dana Sinkler and Alex Dzieduszycki were working for star chef Jean-Georges Vongerichten at his four-star restaurant, Lafayette, in New York when they decided to strike out on their own and start a catering business. They were looking to create a signature dish to serve at the bar since it's the place people first visit at a party. But they wanted something different from the elaborate crudité platters that were popular at the time. So in 1990, they experimented with frying different vegetable roots in the kitchen of Sinkler's tiny apartment and struck gold. The vegetable chips were a hit, and soon the pair brought Terra Chips into stores. In 1995, a private equity group bought 51 percent of the company, and in 1998 Hain Celestial bought Terra Chips as part of an $80 million bundle deal that included three other companies. At the time,

Dzieduszycki says, Terra Chips had $23 million in annual sales.

Rod Johnstone, J/Boats

Rod Johnstone was thirty-eight years old and working as an ad salesman for a boating publication when he decided to design his dream sailboat, one his family of five could enjoy but would still be fast enough to race. His parents donated a few hundred dollars' worth of lumber, and Johnstone started building the boat in his garage. A year and a half later, his dream boat was complete, and he started entering it in races. Johnstone decided to quit his job and turn his dream into his career. That was 1977. Since then, J/Boats has built more than 13,000 boats, from small crafts to yachts, bringing in millions of dollars in revenue. And Johnstone's original design, the J/24, is now in the Sailboat Hall of Fame.

Andy Schamisso, Inko's White Tea

In 2002, Andy Schamisso was working in public relations but wasn't satisfied. One day, when his wife couldn't find the rare, white tea she used for her iced tea, Schamisso found his calling. While searching to buy the tea on the Internet, he discovered its health benefits and decided to bring his wife's recipe to others. So after thirteen years in public relations, Schamisso quit his job to start Inko's White Tea, naming it after his dog. After raising enough money to make 6,000 cases,

Schamisso went up and down the streets of New York selling his product. He eventually branched out into specialty shops. In about a year, orders went from cases to truckloads. There are now fourteen varieties of Inko's White Tea on the market. In recent years, the company has had annual sales of $3 million.

It's easy to look at celebrities as if they are on another level than you, but when you take a real look at how these people came to be where they are, you'll notice that most of them started off just like you and me ... with nothing but a big dream and strong will. Let's take a look:

Jim Carrey used to be homeless.

Carrey revealed to James Lipton on Inside the Actor's Studio *that when he was fifteen, he had to drop out of school to support his family. His father was an unemployed musician, and as the family went from "lower middle class to poor," they eventually had to start living in a van. Carrey didn't let this stop him from achieving his dream of becoming a comedian. He went from having his dad drive him to comedy clubs in Toronto to starring in mega-blockbusters and being known as one of the best actors of an era.*

A shark bit off Bethany Hamilton's arm.

Hamilton started surfing when she was just a child. At age thirteen, an almost deadly shark attack resulted in her losing her left arm. She was back on her surfboard one month later, and a short time after that, there was a movie based on her life.

Stephen King's first novel was rejected thirty times.

If it weren't for King's wife, Carrie *may not have ever existed. After being consistently rejected by publishing houses, King gave up and threw his first book in the trash. His wife, Tabitha, retrieved the manuscript and urged King to finish it. Now, King's books have sold millions of copies and have been made into countless major motion pictures.*

Oprah Winfrey gave birth at age fourteen and lost her child.

She is one of the most successful and richest people in the world today, but Oprah didn't always have it so easy. She grew up in Milwaukee, Wisconsin, and was repeatedly molested by her cousin, uncle, and a family friend. She eventually ran away from home, and at age fourteen gave birth to a baby boy who died shortly after. But Winfrey's tragic past didn't stop her from becoming the force she is today. She excelled as an honors student in high school and won an oratory contest that secured her a full scholarship to college. Now the entrepreneur and personality has the admiration of millions and a net worth of $2.9 billion.

Kris Carr turned her cancer into a business of hope and healing.

In 2003, Karr was a thirty-two-year-old New Yorker just enjoying life. But then, a regular checkup at her doctor's office resulted in a diagnosis of a rare and incurable Stage IV cancer called epithelioid hemangioendothelioma, existing in her liver and lungs. Instead of succumbing to the disease, Carr decided to challenge her diagnosis head-on. She attacked her cancer with a brand new nutritional lifestyle and turned her experience into a series of successful self-help books and documentaries. Eventually, she launched her own wellness website, which is followed by over 40,000 people. Today, Karr is celebrating a decade of "thriving with cancer," and is now revered as one of the most prominent experts on healthy living.

Jay-Z couldn't get signed to any record labels.

Jay-Z came from a rough Brooklyn neighborhood and had dreams to make it big as a rapper. Unfortunately, the rest of the world didn't agree with him at first. Not one record label would sign him. Yet that didn't stop him from creating his own music powerhouse. His label would eventually turn into the lucrative Roc-A-Fella Records. Forbes has estimated his net worth at $500 million, and TIME ranked him as one of their 2013 Most Influential People in the World. He has recently launched the first music streaming company in the world, with the mission of supporting the rights of artists.

Simon Cowell had a failed record company.

By his late twenties, Cowell had made a million dollars and lost a million dollars. Cowell told The Daily Mail in 2012, "I've had many failures. The biggest were at times when I believed my own hype. I'd had smaller failures, signing bands that didn't work, but my record company going bust, that was the first big one." Even after such a momentous loss, Cowell picked himself up and became one of the biggest forces in reality television, serving as a judge for Pop Idol, The X Factor, Britain's Got Talent *and* American Idol. *Forbes has estimated his net worth at $95 million.*

Steven Spielberg was rejected from USC, twice.

One of the most prolific filmmakers of all time, the man who brought us Schindler's List, Jaws, E.T., *and* Jurassic Park *couldn't get into the film school of his choice. In the end, Spielberg would get the last laugh, when USC awarded him an honorary degree in 1994. Two years later, he became a trustee of the university.*

Dreams do come true, if you believe, or at least they do when you get out of your own way and let them happen. My work with the NFL proved it to me over and over again.

Success on any level, whether it be in professional sports, corporate America, the entertainment industry, political endeavors, or those of us who just want to be successful in our careers and family lives, is all about believing nothing is impossible—improbable, maybe, but impossible? Never. This is why no one should ever be allowed to define you. They have no idea what you can really do. Only *you* know that.

Successful individuals achieve as much as they do because of their belief systems, which are based on the core beliefs we all develop early in our lives. Most importantly, these core beliefs can change as we see fit. So if we change our thoughts, we can change our lives. We are the creators of our destiny. If we can imagine it, we can achieve it.

I was told getting into the NFL as a female mental health clinician was impossible, yet I did it. I was told creating a TV series based on my life without an agent or manager was impossible, yet I did it. Those naysayers believed my goals were impossible because they had never seen them done before. But now they, and everyone else, have seen me do the "impossible," and in doing so, I have paved the way for others to do the same, which is why we should never take "no" for an answer. We can literally change reality, for ourselves, and others.

I often think about what Orville and Wilbur Wright must have gone through when they told their friends that they were going to make a flying machine. I'm sure they were laughed at, taunted, and made to feel that they were crazy. But they had each other—their team. And they never stopped, never took *no* for an answer, never got distracted from their dream. Because of that, we fly jets today.

Surround yourself with people that believe in you. It is never too late to change your life circumstances. You are never too old, nor too young, nor too poor, nor too challenged. In fact, I challenge you to succeed. I challenge you to create a life that is amazing. I challenge you to be all that you can be.

I challenge you to believe in your dreams and make the impossible ... possible.

References

George Blanda:
http://www.catalogs.com/info/sports/longest-nfl-football-careers.html

Richard Branson:
http://www.virgin.com/entrepreneur/richard-branson-turn-weakness-strength

Kris Carr
http://www.scientificamerican.com/article/living-with-cancer-kris-carr/

Jim Carrey:
http://newsfeed.time.com/2013/07/11/stars-who-were-once-homeless/slide/jim-carrey/

Simon Cowell
http://www.dailymail.co.uk/home/moslive/article-2114945/Simon-Cowell-Ive-failures-The-biggest-times-I-believed-hype.html

Dr. Donna Dannenfelser
Common Elements Among Successful People Who Are High
School Dropouts, UMI #3122162

Dr. Donna Dannenfelser , Joe Sabatino
A Woman's Guide to the Knuckledragging Sport of
Football, to be released in the fall of 2015

Dr. Donna's Heart Cockles: Heartcockles.com

Dr. Seuss: http://www.catinthehat.org/history.htm

Mike Dooley: Tut.com

Albert Einstein:
http://www.theguardian.com/lifeandstyle/2005/mar/0
2/familyandrelationships.features11

Famous High School Dropouts:
http://www.huffingtonpost.com/2013/06/06/famous-
high-school-dropouts_n_3397652.html

Benjamin Franklin:
http://www.ushistory.org/declaration/signers/franklin.
htm

Bethany Hamilton:
http://en.wikipedia.org/wiki/Bethany_Hamilton

Jay-Z
http://news.bbc.co.uk/2/hi/business/6160419.stm

Stephen King:
http://mentalfloss.com/article/53235/how-stephen-
kings-wife-saved-carrie-and-launched-his-career

Candy Lightner:
http://www2.potsdam.edu/alcohol/Controversies/1119
636699.html

J.K. Rowling: http://www.biography.com/people/jk-
rowling-40998

Colonel Sanders: http://colonelsanders.com/bio.asp

Andy Schamisso, Inko's White Tea:
https://www.mint.com/blog/consumer-iq/people-who-
quit-their-jobs-and-made-millions-022012/

Dana Sinkler and Alex Dzieduszycki, Terra Chips:
http://www.terrachips.com/about-terra-chips/our-
history

Fred Smith:
http://www.referenceforbusiness.com/businesses/A-
F/FedExCorporation.html#ixzz3Ua6xj89r

Steven Spielberg
http://directorsseries.tumblr.com/post/55279069148/s
teven-spielberg-amblin-1968

Rick Wetzel and Bill Phelps, Wetzel's Pretzels:
http://en.wikipedia.org/wiki/Wetzel%27s_Pretzels

Oprah Winfrey
http://www.imdb.com/name/nm0001856/bio

Malala Yousafzai:
http://www.biography.com/people/malala-yousafzai-
21362253

About the Author

Dr. Donna Dannenfelser has been a psychotherapist, certified hypnotherapist, and dream analyst for more than twenty-five years. She started out specializing in women's issues, touring the New York area giving motivational workshops on surviving divorce and separation, parenting issues, substance abuse, physical and verbal abuse, the experience of "coming out" for people who choose to live alternate lifestyles, and coping strategies for survivors of tragic events. Donna soon found herself employed as the mental health clinician for the New York Jets and began specializing in men's issues pertaining to high-profile professional athletes, including their relationships with their wives and families whom she also saw as patients. Her clientele extended to professional athletes from other arenas, such as baseball, basketball, hockey, boxing, wrestling, and golf, along with women's sports such as bodybuilding, dancing, skating, and wrestling.

Eventually, Donna's clientele list included actors, CEOs, and political personalities. This work led to appearances on radio and cable network shows, for which Donna spoke about topics including couples counseling, parenting issues, dream analysis, hypnosis, psychic phenomena, and the power of positive self-talk.

Donna was a professor of Counseling Education at New York Institute of Technology and taught Dream Analysis in the graduate program at SUNY Stony Brook. Donna also served as the Director of Counseling in the New York Public School System and was an adjunct professor at Chapman University in California, teaching psychology in their Education Program.

Donna has been featured as an expert source in magazine articles regarding marital issues and parenting challenges. Her published dissertation, Common Elements Among Successful People Who Are High School Dropouts, is on file at the Library of Congress in Washington, DC. This research project challenged the US educational system on its inability to meet the needs of all children and led to her supervising a million-dollar grant from the US Department of Education to implement counseling services for low-income school districts on Long Island.

In 2006, Donna relocated to southern California, where she continued her private practice, motivational workshops, university teachings, and keynote speaking engagements. She became the founder and CEO of Heart Cockles, Inc. Her website, www.heartcockles.com provides visualization tools and direction to help people find their center and focus on their goals through the Law of Attraction.

Donna then created the television series Necessary Roughness, based on her life as a sports psychologist, for USA Network in collaboration with Sony Pictures Television. Donna served as the Co-Executive Producer for this series, along with earning writer status. The show premiered on June 29, 2011, and aired for three years, winning the Voice Award for mental health awareness in 2012. She is referenced as the real-life sports psychologist behind Callie Thorne's character on Necessary Roughness in the online textbook for the course, Psychology in the Fastlane: Understanding the Human Element.

Dr. Donna's Business

In addition to Dr. Donna being a TV personality, she has a private practice and is a key note speaker about a variety of topics related to mental health and wellness, as well as her own remarkable story of reinvention and success in a variety of external competitive fields. To find her services, visit her website at DrDonnaD.com

If you're looking to learn how to meditate and visualize, and discover the Law of Attraction, visit Dr. Donna's heart cockle website at: Heartcockles.com. Allow Dr. Donna to help you calm yourself and stay focused on your goals through the use of her heart cockles.

Her book, "A Woman's Guide To The Knuckeldragging Sport of Football" will be released in the Fall of 2015.

Connect with the Author

Website: http://www.DrDonnaD.com/

Email: info@DrDonnaD.com

Facebook: www.facebook.com/pages/Donna-Dannenfelser/309348549113369?fref=ts

Linked In: https://www.linkedin.com/pub/dr-donna-dannenfelser/11/43/854

Twitter: @TheDr_Donna

Media

Necessary Roughness, the USA Network drama based on the life of Dr. Donna Dannenfelser, ended its three-season run in November 2013 with an average of four million viewers. During this time, it earned accolades, including a 2012 Golden Globe nomination for star Callie Thorne, and drew recognition for tackling controversial subjects drawn from the real world of professional sports, including illegal performance-enhancing drugs and gay athletes.

The show was the culmination of a longtime fascination with Dr. Donna and her unique role as a female mental health clinician working with an NFL team in the '90s. She has been the subject of frequent profiles, both during the show's run and her years with the New York Jets. Such media attention has included feature articles in *The Wall Street Journal, Newsday,* Oprah's Blog, AOL Jobs, iVillage.com, Entertainment Heartbeat, Health

Bistro, and *The New York Post*, which christened her the Dr. Phil of Sports Psychology, as well as television coverage on ESPN, and radio coverage including, WCGO Radio with Geoff Pinkus, iHeart Radio with Bill Cunningham, The Robert Wuhl Show, Marilu Henner Radio Show, KFI Radio with Lisa Ann Walters, LA Talk Radio, Variety Topics with Sonia Fitch, MYLF Talk Radio with Sophie Venable and Sideshow Radio Network. She has been a frequent talking head on the subject of gay players and homophobia in the NFL, giving interviews for publications including *The Huffington Post*, *Buzzfeed*, Outsports, and *Queerty*.

Dr. Donna regularly appears as an expert guest on television news programs. She was featured on *The Dr. OZ Show*, where she spoke about positive thoughts and how they keep us healthy. She has also joined Regis Philbin on *ESPN's Crowd Goes Wild*, on which she spoke about athletes and their reliance on superstitions. She was featured on *Flipping Out*, as Jeff Lewis' therapist for two seasons. She is also a sports correspondent to *TMZ Sports*, *Bloomberg News*, and the *Today* show. She currently has a blog series for *The Huffington Post*, "Life Is the Ultimate Team Sport."

In addition to being a TV personality, Dr. Donna has a private practice and is a keynote speaker about a variety of topics related to mental health and wellness, as well as her own remarkable story of reinvention and success in a variety of external competitive fields.